Read by:
Joyce H. 7/05
Julie H. 1/19

ALONE

Also by Elizabeth C. Mooney

In the Shadow of the White Plague

ALONE
Surviving as a Widow

Elizabeth C. Mooney

G. P. Putnam's Sons
New York

Copyright © 1981 by Elizabeth C. Mooney
All rights reserved. This book, or parts thereof, must
not be reproduced in any form without permission.
Published simultaneously in Canada by Academic Press
Canada Limited, Toronto.

Library of Congress Cataloging in Publication Data

Mooney, Elizabeth Comstock
   Alone, surviving as a widow.
   1. Widows—United States—Biography.
2. Mooney, Elizabeth Comstock.
3. Bereavement—Psychological aspects.
I. Title
HQ1058.5.U5M66   1981   306.8'8   81-8492
ISBN 0-399-12601-5   AACR2

PRINTED IN THE UNITED STATES OF AMERICA

to my son Ted
who with this book
   assumed the place of his father
as editorial consultant

A man's dying is more the survivors'
affair than his own.
—Thomas Mann,
The Magic Mountain

ALONE

Prologue

IT HAPPENED in the kitchen of the little house in which we had lived together twenty years. Booth was coughing, a prolonged, frighteningly deep coughing spell that went on and on. I replaced the telephone in its cradle and went to stand beside him, put my arms around him. As I did, I saw his hands grip the sink till the knuckles turned white, and a minute later the blood came gushing out of his mouth.

"I'm here," I told him as he sank in my arms to the floor. It was all I had time to say, the only thing I could think of to say before it was over. I sat there with his head cradled in my lap, and I knew there was no hurry to get to the phone for help. "I'm here," I said again stupidly, but I knew he couldn't hear me. He was gone.

When a man to whom you have been married for more than thirty years dies, a piece of you that you will never know again goes out the door with him. Sitting dry-eyed in a chair watching the rescue-squad men load him onto the stretcher and strap him in, I was mercifully numb. Yes, I said obediently, I would await a call from the coroner; yes, his doctor could be reached at the hospital; yes, I would be all right alone.

And then they were wheeling him out the door, casting uneasy backward glances at me. Thirty years of being us was suddenly transformed into just me.

Chapter 1

THE END of a marriage. Who ever considers that her particular marriage should not outlast the tides, the turning of the earth and the statistics? Psychiatrists say it takes two years to accept the fact that you are alone after the end of years of marriage. One of the difficulties is believing it. I was the survivor of an amputation that didn't yet seem real. You never feel the full cut of the knife until later.

Dead. Your husband is dead. You saw him rolled out on a stretcher, you accepted his watch and his wallet and closed the door behind him. You stood in the front pew when they murmured those beautiful sonorous words that tie us all together, all of us who live and die. You put his last shirts in the laundry and you threw out the yogurt he loved and you don't. You know he is dead, but you don't believe it. A part of you can't really accept the fact that he isn't just away on a trip and will be calling to say he'll make the late plane.

I wasn't able to believe it. Asleep or awake, I had trouble believing it. Night after night I woke alone in bed, staring at the ceiling and wondering bleakly where he was. Where do you go when you die? I had asked him once what he thought happened. Nothing, he said. Just nothingness. When I slept, I dreamed repeatedly that we were to meet on a train platform and, though I had caught a glimpse of him earlier, coat over his arm, he didn't appear at the rendezvous. Nightly I got on that train hoping he had boarded earlier, and nightly it pulled out without him.

The children arrived, wept and departed to lives which had not significantly changed. The old dog and I had more apparent holes in our lives. She looked for him in all his accustomed places, staring at his favorite chair and at his bed. Abruptly she gave up. It was a milestone I found hard to bear.

The invitations crowded in on each other, night after night. I accepted compliantly. It didn't matter much to me where I was. They came and got me, brought me back and I put the key in the lock, thanking them like a docile child. The last time I had been so besieged with invitations was the week before our marriage. I came and went, slept and woke, it was all the same to me.

And then the invitations dried up like a brook gone dry in the summer, and everybody went back to his or her own life, to the business at hand. Little by little I realized that ultimately there was now just me. I was alone, and that was how it was to be.

Alone, I discovered, is several different things I had not previously imagined. Alone is having to buck-

yourself up, worry that you will have a heart attack in the bathtub and be found by the police, naked, pathetic and aging, recorded that way forever by the police flash camera. Alone is having to take the sliver out of your own finger, having nobody to pooh-pooh your worries or catch your eye when somebody says something stupid. Alone is panic in the night—who cares anymore, to whom do I matter, whose name will I put in the blank for next of kin? Alone is floating on a raft by yourself in a large ocean, watching the excursion boats steam by full of matched passengers.

I gave myself stern lectures. Life goes on, I said, even if you forget why, and there are things to be done, none of which can be done by anybody else. Maybe it is arranged that way because otherwise you might never get out of bed. The house must be transferred to my name, the bank account looked into, the safety deposit inventoried by a brisk and busy gentleman, the figures prepared for the estate taxes. The huge pile of sympathy notes had to be answered, Booth's office cleaned out. I brought home his ancient, rickety typewriter and his files and put them in the garage, where they looked lonely and too dignified somehow among the bottles of weed killer and half-used paint cans. A lot of figures had to be assessed on the income tax from years back. I surrounded myself with the papers, spread them out over the living-room floor as if I were building a fortress with children's blocks, and pulled the work at hand over my head so I couldn't think.

The children wrote and called frequently, but theirs was a different kind of grief and we all knew it. An old friend of Booth's came to call and confided that the loss of Booth had left him depressed. I stared at him silently, trying to understand that he thought he had said something that linked us, but actually I was furious. What did he know about being left behind?

The kitchen with his body lying on the floor kept crowding back into my mind, but I pushed it away. There would have to come a time when I could look at that sink without seeing his knuckles white as he gripped it for support, but it hadn't yet come. Think about something else.

Ted, our son, came for the weekend, studiously cheerful and watching me anxiously as if I were a flimsily wrapped package that might come apart at the seams. We went to lunch at our favorite Chinese restaurant, and I reassured him over the shrimp roll. I'm fine, just fine, I told him. I thought I was. "When your father died..." I began quite reasonably, gave him a stricken look as I heard the words, put my head in my hands and burst into noisy sobs.

"Mom," he whispered softly from across the table and a million miles away. "Mom." But I sobbed it all out there over the moo-shu pork while our neighbors openly gaped, chopsticks halfway to their mouths. I blew my nose and looked at them angrily. "Kindly chat among yourselves," I told them and went back to my rice.

Somewhere it is written that there is always a reckoning, an appointment in Samarra, that you cannot escape. I was running from grief, and it caught up with me occasionally in odd places. Once at a stoplight when I was caught in traffic, I put my head down on the steering wheel and wept, oblivious to the cacophony of horns behind me. I was driven, scrubbing the kitchen floor at midnight because it was donkey labor and kept me from thinking, writing the thank-you's by the dozen, assembling the endless papers. I was full of contradictions. I filled the house with friends to exorcise the ghosts, but I couldn't touch a thing on the table beside his favorite chair, where his place in the book he was reading remained forever marked with an old letter, and his pipes stood in a neat row in the holder.

I was still winding his watch, and please don't ask me why. Maybe because he wasn't there to do it.

The house seemed full of people who were no longer there, and I kept the lights burning constantly. I tried not to come home until I was too exhausted to care whether I was alone. Frieda, the old dog, met me stiffly at the door, and I decided we were too old and moribund, Frieda and I, and answered an ad in the paper wanting a home for a puppy that had been pushed out of a car at a bus stop.

I knew when I first saw Katie being carried across the street for my approval that she was the wrong dog. She was too big, would require too much from me. She needed a large, exuberant family with children and grandparents and uncles and aunts, all laughing and quarreling, to be loved by and to love. I looked at her outsize paws as she peed on my shoe in excitement, but there was no way I could reject her once I had come that far and we had met. She needed a home, and I needed love. Maybe hers would do. We drove away together, both of us uneasy.

She was black as my despair, with a pair of absurd silver eyebrows, irresistible to look at and a monkey in a china shop in our, no my, suburban garden and house. She could clear the length of the yard in two graceful arabesques, rival the resident squirrels' speed, and she kissed Frieda, who accepted her homage with regal disinterest. At night she cried, shut up alone in the kitchen, so I padded downstairs and took her back up with me, cheek against fuzzy face. I knew how it felt to be alone.

I went out somewhere, anywhere, as often as possible, making up errands if there were none.

"How are you getting along?" inquired a woman sitting across from me at a ladies' fashion luncheon, an invitation which I had accepted because of my new vow to go anywhere no matter how wildly improbable that it would enlarge my life. "Do you know lots of other widows and divorcées?"

I saw, looking at her in stunned disbelief, that it was all there like a lesson for me to learn. She had taken it for granted that I knew. The world has its rules, it is geared to pairs, to balanced numbers and married couples, and the misfits had better understand early that if they want to enjoy the rest of their lives, they should seek friendship among their own kind.

And the worst of it was that I could remember when I too had avoided the unbalanced dinner table as I avoided somebody with a particularly nasty head cold. I shook my head angrily, not because of her simple acceptance of the modern version of Indian suttee but because I was remembering a me that used to be. I too had once believed that, as on the Ark, people are acceptable only two by two. It was different now that it was me.

At home Kate and Frieda and I lived our unmatching existence, ate our solitary meals—Kate on the back porch, Frieda in the kitchen and I, like the Englishman dressing for dinner in the jungle, alone at the dining-room table with the candles lit, reading. Seventeen million people live alone, but it doesn't make you feel any better to know it. I have an acquaintance who, for weeks after her husband died, sat on the floor with her poodle to eat. Anything more complicated wasn't worth the effort. I was determined to do better. There was some comfort in doing everything just as I always had, a certain subcutaneous invisible strength to be derived from being able to cope with the demands of everyday life.

But there were plenty of things I wasn't ready to face. Weeks went by before I could as much as open Booth's closet and look at the suits hanging in neat rows, suits that he would never again need. They were useless to Ted. He was built from a different last. He had given them a brief glance, shaken his head and departed with a single army shirt from World War II, that distant war which has its own cachet among the young. It was up to me to give them to somebody who needed them.

In the end I had to get a little drunk to do it. I poured myself a drink of whiskey neat, strong enough to burn my throat, and paused while it made its painful, burning progress to my stomach. I coughed and waited while it made itself at home, radiating feelers of comfort and encouragement. When I put the glass down, I knew I could do it.

A faint, unmistakable smell of Booth lingered there, part tobacco, part shave lotion, part just him. I could see the brown tweed jacket in which he had died hanging there still in the cleaner's bag in which it made the journey home after heroic efforts at the hands of an expert to remove the blood. Friends had brought that jacket home in a paper bag from the hospital, where they had taken him briefly after it was all over, spoken earnestly with dry-cleaning clerks about how to remove the blood. I could no longer remember why it was so important to me to have that jacket return to his closet. I looked at it a long time and then gathered it and all its neighbors into my arms and lugged them downstairs and into the car. It took me four trips to do it, dropping shoes and neckties and belts along the way, but I stuffed them all in, slammed the door and drove, abstracted and dry-eyed, to the nearest Salvation Army collection point. The man gave me a bored look and a neat pink slip in exchange for the last bits and pieces of Booth's life.

It was a step toward healing, but I couldn't shake the slightly drunken feeling that I had gotten rid of part of him. I moved my winter clothes into the empty closet and took Katie for a long walk.

I decided not to touch the things beside his chair.

Chapter 2

GOD KNOWS I loved him, but he did a lousy job of preparing me to be a widow.

I loved him with the fierce abandon that was part of the love affairs of 1944, when everybody was in uniform and the country was united like a close family and the future was dictated by tomorrow's headlines. Standing naked in hotel bedrooms, he would peer down at me with solemn dignity and shake his head. "If this doesn't last," he would mutter, "I will never believe in anything again." And he would put on his Army Air Force captain's hat, cocking it over one eye rakishly, naked as a jaybird below the visor, and grin at me.

"It'll be all right for us," he promised.

And I knew it would be.

I knew it would outlast the stars and Hitler and his

current marital obstacles, and I knew I would have walked barefoot over glass for him. I thought the cigarette dangling from the corner of his mouth insouciant and rakehell. We were very young, and everything was possible.

He took me out of the small town where I was born and showed me a world that was wider and very much less secure, but I never doubted that he would bring it to heel. He was starting his own business, and he had guest cards to several clubs, but there was no furniture in our little house and no food. No refrigerator, no stove, no tables, no chairs, no nothing. We gave a party and everybody sat on the floor and thought it was amusing.

I knew that he would provide and everything would be okay. And when it was, I wasn't in the least surprised.

But even though, toward the end, he would look at me sadly and murmur, "I am training you to be a widow," it was not true. No one was ever less trained to be a widow. When I was rushed, he had written my newspaper stories; in his sleep he tossed and flailed about, beseeching me not to worry, everything would be all right. He held my hand, took care of me, reassured me, made the decisions, called me, for God's sakes, Baby. It was another life, another world, which had brainwashed us all into believing that marriage is woman's destiny and that is all that need be said.

My life was tuned to his and, without him, the focus flickered out like a burnt match. I had to start all over again, learning to walk alone. And one of the first things I learned was that I had to help everybody else get adjusted to what had happened, too.

I was passing the phone in the hall when it rang, and I turned to answer it. The voice on the other end belonged

to the son of an old friend who lived in a distant city.
"Hello, Mrs. Mooney."
"Hello, Fred. How are you?"
"Gee, I'm fine. How are you?"
"Getting along pretty well." (Booth is now dead three weeks.) "How's your dear mother?"
"Oh, she's fine. You know her. She's always busy about something."
"Fine. That's a good thing." (In fact, it's the only way to keep alive.)
"Yes." (Pause.) "How're the children?"
"They seem to be getting along all right."
Pause.
"Fred, you *did* know Booth is dead, didn't you?"
Uncomfortable pause.
"Yes. That's why I'm calling."

Every widow hears a version of this conversation, learns the lesson enclosed within. What has happened to her is very depressing and very embarrassing for everybody else because no one knows what to say.

The whole world is nervous about the new widow. It knows a terrible thing has happened, it wants to say something suitably kind, but everything seems inadequate. The result is some of the most unreal dialogue heard outside the high-school drama-club workshop. There is plenty of pity, plenty of sympathy, but mostly there is fear that they'll have a weeping woman on their hands who will make a scene that will embarrass everybody. Consequently people tend to babble about anything at all but the central fact obsessing your mind, rather the way you avoid looking at the stump of a new amputee.

Widows as a class have the image of life's losers. Even in the printer's world, a widow is something left over from the last line that nobody can figure out what to do with. The conspiracy is to pretend that nothing has really happened, or if it did, better not to refer to it again. Nobody cares to consider the death because it reminds them of their own inevitable demise, and certainly the less thought given *that* the better. Only the three days between the death and the funeral are allotted to the widow to work it out. After that, if she wants to be a part of the life she knew before, she had better shape up. Death in our time has been reduced to a regrettable but brief incident which doesn't bear talking about.

My old friend, Carol, was in town for a day or two a few weeks after Booth's death and called to say she'd like to take me to lunch. Nothing could have pleased me more, for Carol and I were friends when we were both first married, when the children were babies and we ate grilled sandwiches on the porch, leaning over the Scrabble board, dropping crumbs and studying the tiles until our bones ached. We were easterners together in the capital of the Southwest, outlanders in a strange world, a bond which has withstood the test of separation. When she comes, I promised myself, I will tell her everything, how it happened and how I didn't understand he was so sick and was even planning to go out. She will say nothing I could have done would have changed how it ended and I will believe her, because Carol does not say things to make people happy.

It was a tearful reunion, and I led her to the sofa for a prelunch sherry. She accepted the glass and settled back in that room in which we spent so many evenings, we two with our husbands.

"What will your daughter be doing this summer?" she inquired.

It is perfectly understandable. Nobody to whom it has

not happened can possibly understand your need to relive what has happened until you can exorcise it. The last thing that occurs to friends is that you even want to think about it again. But the whole scene of the last moments is stuck somewhere in your throat, undigested in your mind after weeks, taken out of its wraps only in your unconscious moments.

Your entire world has just crumbled, the future is one big question mark, you haven't gotten used to the fact that you are alone—you don't even believe it—and there is a widespread conspiracy to divert you to think about something else. I was walking through a bad dream from which I was not going to wake, and everybody on all sides was telling me what movie I should see, where the best lamb chops could be bought. What I was thinking was, one true love to a customer and I've had mine. I knew my life was over, and they wanted me to consider what restaurant would be best for lunch.

Like a compliant child, I did my best to please them, but left alone I slipped back into reruns of the terrible scene in the kitchen. In bed I lay sleepless, wincing as I remembered asking him to take the trash out only two days before he died. By day I forced the private movies into the shadows, forbidding myself to dwell on the fact that I could have gotten the doctor quicker, should have demanded a specialist months ago, should have seen how things were going downhill.

Chin up. Everybody was proud of me.

"Come to dinner," Alexia's voice on the phone would say, and I would get into the car and go over, as I had for so many years, to eat with her and George, who had been an old friend of Booth's. Alexia is not the kind of a person who would neglect anybody who needed her. Elegant little dinners with George's carefully chosen wine, chitchat about nothing much, solicitous questions. I ate and drank obediently, went home alone at ten, not forgetting to lock the car doors. I locked them because I promised George I would, and promises were to be kept. The fear of rape and murder had receded to the very bottom of my worry list.

There was really nobody I could talk it out with. No tears, no dwelling on the past because it's over now. But the truth is, it was scarcely beginning. What they don't tell you is that it gets harder after a while. I was nobody's brave soul—I was simply preoccupied, still dazed by what lay behind and in front of me. I was functioning underwater in a strange, semi-real world. Once I locked myself out and stood looking at the locked door dully. Whether I was in or out was not a matter of great moment, but things were expected of you. I broke the window with a brick, feeling like an intruder in my own life.

I forgot invitations, put the spatula in the deep freeze and the ice cream in the pantry shelf. I padded downstairs in my bare feet thinking I had forgotten to turn down the heat. One day I spent the entire morning looking for my glasses, and when at last I gave up and decided to order a new pair, discovered them on my nose. I couldn't read a book—it required too much of my mind, where most of the cylinders were missing.

Nights when I woke I wondered why I had been chosen to have this happen to me. Nobody else I knew was a widow. All the rest were half of a pair, their lives ticking along like fine Swiss watches. I thought about it every night when I turned on the lights for the evening. One out of six over the age of twenty-one is a widow, but not one within my ken. Out there somewhere in the city were hundreds of thousands of husbands, catching buses, retrieving cars from monthly pay parking lots, fighting traffic to come home to women who were even now laying two places at the dinner table, putting clean towels in the bathroom, hanging clean shirts in closets. But not me.

None was a widow, but some understood.

"Could I come for a weekend?" said the voice of my childhood friend, Minor, across the long-distance wires.

"Do come," I answered apathetically. It didn't even register that she was flying more than a thousand miles to me, asking herself because I could not supply the volition to ask her myself, wrapping me in friendship I wasn't even able to recognize.

Not much of her visit remains with me. It was too soon after what had happened, and things at this stage simply swept over me. Only I remember her sitting at my little kitchen table, listening as I talked to someone who held a financial key to my future, I can't remember who. All I can recall is the frustration and the feeling that the whole world conspired against me, had chosen me as the fall guy, had united to deprive me of everything I loved, to keep me from getting what I needed. Somewhere in the course of the conversation, I exploded into deep-seated, enormously wronged anger, banged the telephone down and turned to Minor, shaking. There she sat, looking troubled, sympathetic and a little scared, but also secure and untouched by what had hit me in an avalanche, and for a moment her undamaged world infuriated me.

"They're all gunning for me," I sobbed. "Everything is up to me, and I can't do it all. It's too much. He had no right to kill himself with cigarettes," I howled, and every psychiatrist in the country would have loved the textbook-perfect scene. "What did he think I was going to do without him?"

It was therapeutic, but Minor was looking at me stricken, and I was ashamed.

"It's okay," I said, turning away from her sympathy. "I'm all right."

It was a very large lie.

I was ashamed, but actually I shouldn't have been. It is a common reaction, but I didn't realize it then. Not, maybe, until I met Maria.

Where did I meet Maria? Not though the old channels; possibly through one of those gatherings at which I found myself because people prodded me to go out, get out of the house. Come to the autograph party, the traffic-committee meeting, the school fair. It will do you good, keep you in the world. I only remember looking up and meeting a pair of steady brown eyes staring at me quizzically.

"Do you always stir your coffee with a fork?" she asked.

I shrugged. Fork, spoon, whatever; no matter. But we were for a moment an isolated island of two in a crowd, trying to be civil to each other. Whatever we were attending swirled around us, and I studied her out of the corner of my eye. Late twenties, obviously intelligent, self-contained, keeping a motherly eye on a small child in the corner who was reading a book.

No, her husband was not there. Actually, he was dead, had died at the wheel of the car taking the baby-sitter home. Only a little while earlier she had adopted his two children, five and eight, whose own mother had died suddenly. Well, yes, it was difficult, had always been, because she also had the fifteen-month-old baby. But she was carrying on.

Well, were there moments . . . ?

Sure, there were moments, but it was better now. There *had* been a watershed moment. And as strangers on a train who will never see each other again will tell the intimate details of their lives, she told me what had happened. It was when she was calling the children in for dinner.

She stirred her coffee and looked inward.

"I was pretty stalwart," she said. "Everybody said so. Mother and father to the children, keeping their lives as much as possible the way they were before. It was bad when the baby kept calling every man who rang the doorbell Dada, but she forgot it after a while. And then that night I went to the door and called, but they didn't come in right away.

"I guess something just crumpled. And all of a sudden my knees gave way and I sagged down the side of the wall to the floor and just lay there, sobbing hysterically. When they came in and stood in a circle staring down at me round-eyed, all I could get out through the sobs was, 'I can't do it alone unless you help me.'"

She looked at the child in the corner for a moment and then back at me.

"Which is your husband?" she said.

But I turned away to hide the tears in my eyes. For the first time I had discovered that I was not truly alone.

Chapter 3

THERE IS nothing as instructive as a simple balance sheet with income and outgo neatly laid out side by side and the difference written in red. I was working my way through the papers, and the message was everywhere the same. I was fifty-seven years old, owner of a nice house in an expensive neighborhood whose taxes I couldn't afford, two mongrel dogs and a bank account with $264 in it. Unless I figured out some way to augment the income I could expect, I would be left with a pocketful of charge plates at places like Bergdorf and Neiman Marcus, champagne tastes and an income close to the official poverty level.

"There isn't any money," I told my daughter, Joan, in the surprised and vaguely distressed tone I used to use when we were halfway through making a batch of cookies and discovered we didn't have enough flour.

I might as well have said it looked like rain. The words had no meaning for her. The young brought up in comfortable homes during the sixties long ago adopted the trappings of poverty as a protest against having been handed the comforts of life. Being broke didn't have the same meaning for her. Besides, she had a job; a summer job, it is true, but a job. She was very adept at hiding the shame of her suburban background and dancing schools with blue jeans and bus schedules. She was free, independent if you didn't count room and board, and hand-to-mouth happy. Insurance, taxes and gas bills were not part of her thinking.

She looked at me sympathetically and went on reading the paper. Broke or not, she could see nothing had changed. I was talking about abstracts.

One or two old friends, however, could imagine I might be short, though I am sure they assumed it was only temporary.

"Can I lend you some money?" inquired an old acquaintance diffidently, taking me aside in the kitchen while the chitchat went on in the living room. I shook my head. Well, then maybe, he went on, pouring himself a drink from the Chivas Regal bottle into which I had secretly decanted the cheapest Scotch I could buy, I ought to consider selling the house.

I could hear the sound of his words echoing and reechoing inside my head as I watched him down the Scotch. It was one of those moments frozen forever in memory, in which you can remember just how the sun hit the pattern of the linoleum and what everybody concerned was wearing. I waited until he put the glass down, and then I kicked him hard in the shins and put my head down on the sink and bawled.

The one thing I knew for sure, sobbing disgracefully into the sink's porcelain bosom, was that if I had to burn the Queen Anne dining room chairs one at a time to keep the house warm, if I had to solicit on Broadway to buy the food, I was not going to sell the house. It was not a decision I made on the spot. It was something I seemed always to have known.

I knew at the time I was flying in the fact not only of logic but of the American way. Selling the house is the sensible thing to do, one of the predictable landmark things to do, as taken for granted as the flight of the children and their metamorphosis into holiday guests. The house, a small one with a pocket-size garden and some big trees, would have made possible solvent Golden Years. It was my ticket to a future with no attic or basement and a father figure of an apartment manager on whom I could lay my mechanical domestic problems.

Never.

I said it often, through my teeth, as they kept asking. The house was my Tara, and I would fight for it. It was where I had been happy, where we had all been young. Frieda, now so old and lame, had scampered through its rooms as a frisky puppy. A chipmunk living under the woodpile had grown to count on me for handouts of unroasted peanuts. The front door still bore scars inflicted with a hammer by Ted at three in a losing battle with a recalcitrant latch. Every room in that house was full of household ghosts. Where would they go if I sold?

"Yes, I'll be staying where I am," I told the neighbors who inquired. After a while I learned not to bare my teeth when I said it.

The children and their coterie have, I've noticed, an odd generational loyalty. Pass a remark about any of their friends and their habits, and they will leap to the defense of the accused with the party line. "What's wrong with being an ova-lactic vegetarian?" they will demand fiercely. "Why should she have to change the sheets on her bed every week or two? It's a long way to the Laundromat."

It makes them shake their heads to hear that those of us who were young when Bloomingdale's was tacky didn't all have jobs. Self-appointed for the defense, I offer excuses that should not be alien to them. I and my sisters were children of our generation, the last to honor parental mores. We were taught, until World War II exploded all accepted ideas, that if we had a job, it was not only all right but *demanded* of us to resign when the diamond sparkled on our third finger. We got married and quit, mostly because we were raising them. We thought that would be enough. Only some of us know different now.

Even if we had a job, it was in another life when you couldn't fail; the ground rules were all in our favor. They needed us, employers were begging for us. We were the first wave of women stepping up for paychecks—the first women reporters, the first women line foremen; we were all they could get and they were happy to have us. Rosie the Riveter; Jane Arden, the girl reporter; mechanics, photographers, paramedics; we were the first. Barriers were crashing everywhere while the men were off fighting the war. Doors that never before had been open were swinging wide. If we wanted it then, the world was ours. The trouble was we didn't know we had options.

We knew, or we thought we knew, that everything stopped short at the altar in the final fadeout after we had traded it all in for love. We watched Rosalind Russell and Kay Francis do this in the movies, and we read it in all the magazines. We knew it was proper to take our identities from our husbands. We, the wives of bank clerks, or insurance agents or lawyers, took our position in the world from them. While our daughters know they will sink or swim on their own, we didn't live in a world like that.

We had our cigarettes lit, were helped into our overshoes, assisted into cars, and our tacit acceptance of all this marked us as—God, how long has it been since anyone used the word except on the doors of public rest rooms?—ladies. The men we married took over our lives, took care of the insurance and the taxes and the greasing of the automobile and the unsticking of windows. We were the last generation to enter into the bargain—"you earn the money and I'll make the home." Our husbands, as a matter of course, provided. The world, including us, expected them to. We didn't even inquire too closely how they did it. It was men's work, it was their business. Our province was the home.

But here I was, coming out from under the hammer blow of shock into a world where the rules had suddenly gotten changed. Dimly I was beginning to understand that everything from the inflation of the automobile tires to the income-tax figures was entirely up to me. Nobody was even going to point out that it was time to do what had to be done. And the money available was clearly not going to meet the expenses.

"I'm going to have to look for a job," I said to Alexia. "I don't like being poor. I am not good in the role of poor little match girl. I've got to find some way of laying hold of some money."

Alexia never says blunt things—except when she's very angry—and she certainly would never point out that this might be difficult. She looked at me for a while and then put down her coffee cup and stared off into space.

"I had a wonderful job once," she said thoughtfully.

"George had to ask the receptionist if I would see him." She picked up her cup, sank back against the pillows and looked at me. "They wouldn't hire me to sweep out the Salvation Army now."

I knew she was right. The want ads didn't seem to be looking for me.

But there was that middle-aged clerk—who had surely had her secure clerical job forever, including two weeks with pay—bending over the tax roll out in the county assessor's office, bringing closer and closer the inevitable moment when a tax bill would be pushed through my mail slot.

Thinking about her was the beginning of my metamorphosis.

The first time I noticed it was when they gave me too much change in the Safeway. I was wearing my best clothes, ready to go to a luncheon, and eight cents was involved. I knew I was going to point out the error, but the words got stuck in my throat. I walked out to the car as guilty as if I'd been shoplifting and not yet apprehended. Somehow it had turned into a part of my survival—the Safeway or me. It was symbolic of my new way of life. I was no longer part of a class tuned to noblesse oblige, but a brand new card-carrying member of screw-'em-if-you-can. It seemed a watershed moment, and I walked away appalled.

I became extremely conscientious about not leaving a light on in a room in which I was not. I pushed down the heat till I was cold all the time. I clipped cents-off coupons from the paper, congratulating myself that I was paying for the cost of the subscription. I reduced the dogs to no-frills dog food, which they seemed not to distinguish from the more expensive spread. At the end of the week, petty thrift had so shriveled my soul and depressed my mind that I went out and bought an expensive blouse. I ate tuna fish for three days to make up for it and then had to take Frieda to the vet, which blew any saving. I painted the front door myself, sanity returning only just in time to keep me from ascending a ladder and cleaning the gutters of leaves. I was obsessed with cutting expenses.

Meanwhile I was listening to the same conversations I had always listened to.

"We're not going back to Antigua this year. Harry can't get away in February and that's the time to go to Antigua. I think we'll go to the south of France in April."

Nothing had changed but me. Sitting in my chair, affecting polite interest, I was choking back class anger. I was getting a crash course in how the French Revolution came about, and it scared me. It wasn't that I wanted to go to Antigua or the south of France, but my desire to be able to pay my taxes on the house was akin to religious fervor. I promised myself that the masses would overthrow the system and wished my rich friends bad weather in April so hard I was afraid they could read it in my face.

At the gas station I grew very adept at the self-service island, feinting to defend my place in line, wrestling the snakelike pump line to the ground with a practiced foot. I could check the oil and add my own, bought cheap at the Safeway; change the furnace filters; unscrew the chandelier globes and install new bulbs. I could open all but the most recalcitrant screw tops, which I saved and took with me to parties for husbands of friends to open. Trying to open the difficult tops, I often had to swallow a lump in my throat. It embodies everything that never had been but was now up to me.

It rained hard, the basement flooded and I descended with my mop and bucket, sloshing about in water up to my ankles, mopping till my back seemed permanently bent. Poor brave me, I was thinking, which of course was utter nonsense. I would have been doing exactly the same thing if Booth had been alive. He would have been at work when I discovered it or he would have mopped awhile beside me, straightened up and said it was madness to kill ourselves, it would recede. He was not a man who took kindly to floor mopping. Alone, I felt the onus of the Dutch boy with his finger in the dike.

I was disciplining myself as best I could, and sometimes I thought I was getting better at it. No longer did I quail at a large cocktail party; I downed a drink and stepped up to the first likely-looking group. I can't say it was fun, but it was part of the program I had outlined for myself. And at one of these I met an acquaintance I had not seen in some time.

She peered speculatively at me over the rim of her glass and announced I was looking well.

It was one of those remarks people trot out when nothing else occurs to them, but I took it personally, an accolade, a merit badge earned by not allowing myself to become a frump. Somehow it seemed important, and I preened a bit.

But she was still staring at me.

"You're tough, aren't you?" she said in the same tone in which one might observe that the weather is warming up.

I looked at her aghast. My growing image of myself as a resourceful, competent female faded like the Cheshire cat's grin before her steady gaze. I felt like a schoolgirl reprimanded in chapel.

She must, of course, not know this.

"Yes," I told her, "tough and getting tougher." And we parted company en route to the hors d'oeuvres.

Afterward, staring owl-eyed at the bedroom ceiling, her words kept going round in my head. Ah, to see ourselves as others see us. Tough, was it? Yes, tough—but not hard. I hoped there was a difference.

After a while I turned on the light again and padded downstairs in my bare feet, ignoring the sleeping dogs, making a pilgrimage through every room of the house. There was my mother's picture on the wall in the library. She was no help. She died before my father. What did she know about stumbling on alone? I sat down in the easy chair and stared at the needlepoint footstool I had spent long, happy hours making. No time for that kind of thing anymore. Needlepoint is for minds at peace, fingers filling up hours.

I went back to the kitchen and made myself a cup of tea. Drinking it, looking around the room, I recognized it for what it was—a foxhole. So why not? I would defend it, keep everything as much as possible the way it was before I lost my passport to how it used to be.

Widow. I said the word over to myself, sipping my tea thoughtfully. A word with very poor connotations. Ask half the world for free association and they'd come up with a lot of things I didn't want—loneliness, gray hair, dependence on grandchildren and Walter Cronkite, bridge, matinees, fear.

It wasn't going to be that way with me. I meant to lick all the stereotypes, even insolvency.

But what was the struggle doing to *me* along the way?

Chapter 4

I was having trouble sleeping—in fact, sleep was impossible. I decided to wander about in the safe past, take a look at the library of my hometown in my mind, lie on my back looking up through the pines in my grandmother's wild-flower garden. I tried mentally walking through every room in the house where I was born, picking up and examining every object. The silver dish where we kept the keys on the hall table under the gold mirror, the old brass letter opener with the dragon on the handle, the striking clock now downstairs on my own mantel, at present sick and awaiting a trip to the clock man who thinks he can fix it. "If I had known, I would have waited to come until after it was fixed," Ted had said. Things the way they were matter in our family.

I was still sleepless. I built fantasies of winning the lottery and the places I would go and the things I would buy with the loot. Acapulco, probably. I always wanted to see Acapulco. And Nassau. I never got there, either. And while I'm about it, a face-lifting, or maybe a new face, so that I could drive men mad. And a new battery for the car. What are the chances of winning the lottery if you buy a ticket only every other week? What are the chances, for that matter, of ever falling asleep? Who was that doctor I sat next to at a dinner once who claimed to be a sleep expert and said that when insomniac nights build back-to-back, you should take a sleeping pill to throw a roadblock into gathering panic? But there hadn't been a sleeping pill in this house since that night that now seems so long ago that I would rather not think about it.

I plumped the pillow and forbade the things lurking on the edges of my mind to enter. If he died broke, he must have known it all along, must have had that to bear in addition to being terminally sick. And not one word to me. Right to the end he never leaned on me, protected me from how it was.

It was no use. I sat up in bed and turned on the light, banishing things that hide in the shadows. There was the old dressing gown on the chair, the one I wore that terrible night, and in spite of everything I could do it all came flooding back. Two o'clock, said the little clock on the dresser. In my mind it is frozen at ten minutes past ten, as it was that night. I put my hands over my ears against the sound of his labored breathing, squeezed my eyes shut against the sight of the note on the floor just there between the beds.

I sat, like an observer at a play, and watched myself sink to my knees on the floor beside him, sobbing that all the reports are not yet in, why had he done it?

None of this was useful, and I adjured myself not to think of that night again. I got up and went downstairs, turning on all the lights the way I did that night when the whole house was ablaze as if for a party. "You'll know the house by the lights," I told the doctor at five the next morning, when I knew he would not after all die, had not taken enough pills. But in between had been the long long night alone when I had honored what he asked me to do as I had promised him I would. I had not lifted a finger to call him back, had waited for him to die, and he had been given back to me for two more months.

I had thought then that I would never be as alone again. Maybe I was wrong. But you don't die of loneliness.

The sound of Katie's tags jingling as she crept downstairs to see what I was doing made me turn. She stood looking at me from the doorway and then came and laid her head in my lap. He never knew her; they passed each other in my life without meeting. Well, if he could bear what he had to bear, I could survive now.

I'd think of some way to do it.

> Entry level pos. in nutritional activist organ. Typing, filing, share the general office work. Will train. Biology degree pref. Modest salary.

> Once-in-a-lifetime change for bright, agress, yg person on way up. Adv. deg. pref, expertise in computer program. or math major helpful.

It was June, and the ads were singing the annual siren song to the young on the way up. However much I needed the money, they were still not looking for me.

Each time I got to the end of the classifieds, I drew a breath of mingled desperation and relief. Stepping back into the work force after a gap of thirty years was a little like going off the high board when you've been watching the kids in the wading pool.

Meanwhile Joan was graduating from Vassar and would be coming home at least for a while to live with me until she saved some money. Beside this news, everything paled. No longer would the house echo with what I didn't want to think about. I would have somebody to eat with again, somebody to tie up the telephone line, run the stereo loud behind closed bedroom doors, help walk the dogs. And yes, share expenses.

Graduation is one of those bittersweet occasions that call back the memories, and the extra bed in the motel room reserved so long ago undid me. But there is nothing so therapeutic as the lovely, muddled, messy, heedless world of the young, and I was swept up in it, picnicking on the grass under the trees, staggering up and down a thousand stairs with stuffed packing boxes, trying to stow four years' accumulation of Joan's life into the little Ford, drinking sentimental toasts to the future in toothbrush glasses destined to be left behind. In the long line of graduates I picked her out with my opera glasses and discovered she was barefoot under the cap and gown. The speaker droned on and, through it all, I could hear Booth saying so long ago as she opened her acceptance, "I always wanted to have a Vassar daughter."

And then it was all over, preserved forever in the Instamatic: the barefoot girl graduate, the diploma and the student loan for the last year.

"I'm terribly broke," I said to Joan over our eternal

cups of tea in the kitchen. "Terribly, fundamentally without funds."
She looked at me speculatively across the generations. "That's a Calvin Klein dress," she said. "You bought strawberries. This is a very nice house. What do you mean, broke?"
I thought about it, my mind doing the best it could with rust in the engine. Emotionally bankrupt, pretty unable to cope still, scared. Not of having to apply for food stamps but of not being able to support the house which was so necessary to me, my life raft in a crazily shifting world, my continuity in a frightening new life. "I won't budge from here till I die," I could hear my ninety-two-year-old Aunt Marjorie's cracked voice insisting as she traded a load of coal for the eighteenth-century highboy and the grandfather clock for an aluminum walker. I'll be the same, I thought; maybe we're all the same. I didn't even feel apologetic about it.
But that was too complicated to explain.
"Just broke," I said. "*Nouveau pauvre*. I don't look broke because they haven't caught up with me yet and I escaped with some of the things I already had. Tomorrow will be different. Do you think I could ask for a contribution every week? Not board and room, you understand, just another adult sharing?"
She said she had always meant to do that, and I believed her.
She got a temporary job working in a bookstore and, though it was lovely to see her records and books and dirty socks lying around, I saw very little else of her. With time on my hands, I went back to worrying.
All the people in the neighborhood had their houses painted for the season. Some of them had their furnaces and fireplaces cleaned. The painter came around and

rang my doorbell, asking if, as long as he was in the neighborhood, I didn't want him to do mine, too. "How much would it be?" I asked him. He walked around the house several times, writing down little figures on a note pad, and then rang the doorbell again.

"Twelve hundred dollars," he said.

I burst into tears, and he went away looking frightened.

The tax bill dropped through the mail slot with an almost noiseless plop that echoed like trumpets in the pit of my stomach. I hunched myself over it, filling out the forms asking for poverty-income dispensation, dipped into the dwindling savings for the rest. Really scared by now, I called up an old friend of Booth's and asked him if he could help me find a job. He said he hadn't known I needed one and would be back in touch. I never heard from him again.

Outwardly my life continued as before, and only I knew how shaky were the underpinnings. I was still playing bridge and golf as if I were a suburban matron, but the gulf between me and my partners yawned and widened.

When I said I was looking for a job, they looked at me curiously. What kind of job? Jobs were not part of their lives, except as held by husbands.

"You could sell clothes at Saks," suggested Ruth, who spends a good deal of time at Saks by choice. Ruth likes things nice, and Saks is nice. If you have to work, best to have nice carpets underfoot. Ruth has never worked and never will.

"Be a checker at the Safeway," suggested Harriet, who orders her groceries from a specialty store. "Mindless and good pay."

And they fell to arguing whether they should plant pansies in the fall or buy them full grown in the spring when you could be sure of their color. Seedlings get mismarked. So much for career choices.

"I paid the property taxes last week," I told Joan as I dished out the hamburgers that night. "They can't come and take the house away for another year."

"Um," she said, salting her hamburger. She was not really paying attention. She was stirring her tea and searching for words. She was in love. She would be going to Paris to live for a while. It was all arranged. She had the money now for the ticket. Would there be enough money for me to come over for a visit?

It was a shock, but I seemed somehow to have always known it was coming. At twenty-two love is like lightning, always hovering on the horizon, ready to tip the balance, change the world, the future, everything. What is moving to a new country if you are in love? Just a fillip, as trying on a new hat used to be for my mother. I felt depressed.

I was born in the wrong era. In a world in which everybody changes cities, not to mention houses, as easily as slipping into another pair of shoes, I have lived in only three cities and four houses in my life and was dragged kicking and looking back over my shoulder from every one except my father's when I married. The place in which I am living is not a temporary convenience to me, a base from which to spring. It is central, it is all. But without Joan, now that I had gotten used to having her home again, my house was going to seem like a shell.

But leaning on the children is the cardinal sin. It is written somewhere in letters of fire that we must let them go where opportunity or love or money or madness beckons, their roots permanently wrapped for transplanting, citizens of the world. Joan must not be allowed to imagine that I did anything but rejoice at her news, which was so exciting for her. Wave good-bye from the shore, especially since you can't do anything else and it's better to do it with good grace. I knew the young man. I had never imagined that he would not come to her rather than she to him.

I swallowed the lump in my throat and the returning feeling that life had conspired to thwart me.

"Of course I'll come," I said at once. "I'll get a job afterward."

Chapter 5

WHO KNOWS why, when you have lost the person most dear to you, you do the things you do? The mind that seemed to be clicking along as usual is operating with a skeleton staff, reason has taken leave of absence and you haven't even been notified. You're a creature of whim, and if you think about it at all, you are rather proud of it. Here I am, you say to nobody in particular, doing all these things I might have thought twice about before. I must be adjusting, you say; you even feel a trifle exultant.

I was far from adjusting. The last thing in the world I should have done was take any money out of the evaporating savings and fly to Paris.

I knew it. But I didn't care. I had learned that things change very quickly, fall away under your feet. The world cannot be counted on. I wanted to go, and I was going. I would, of course, do it on the cheap.

"I think I'm going to Paris," I volunteered sheepishly over the phone to Alexia, offering unasked for information in a way she would never dream of doing. "I'm going to do it on the cheap. Joan is finding me some run-down hotel."

Alexia made agreeable sounds and pretended that she thought this the best of all possible ideas. She is a woman of consummate taste and would never consider suggesting that I couldn't afford it. She said at once that she thought the trip would do me good and she would drive me to the airport.

We glossed over what Joan was doing in Paris. You do not tell Alexia things she would rather not know, such as that the world is different from when we grew up, and not every love affair today has been sanctioned by clergy.

We talked a good deal more, and I was hanging up with the totally unreasonable feeling that she should have told me I was crazy to go, when she murmured sweetly:

"Have you thought what you'll do at night if Joan is busy? A tray in your room?"

"You'll be all right, won't you?" asked Ted.

He was waving good-bye to me at the East Side Terminal after a brief visit and a farewell binge in the city. As the bus revved up to lumber into the midnight rain for JFK International, I reflected that this question was just about the only one I get asked anymore.

"Certainly," I said stoutly. But I had never felt less all right, at least for a long time. There was absolutely no earthly reason why I couldn't spend ten days in Paris without spending a packet of money and still enjoy myself. I would be seeing Joan again, get to look at where she was living. Then why were the tears behind my glasses getting mixed up with the rain on the windowpanes? Suddenly, inside that lurching bus, sanity returned and I wanted to shout Stop right here, let me off, I have made a terrible mistake. I should be at home studying the want ads instead of winging across a cold gray ocean in the dark on an economy plane.

Write it in your copybook ten times—economy is easier when you are young. When you are not young, economy suggests after a while this is the way it will always be and you'd better get used to it. When you are young, you know that you will lick the world and that inconvenience is temporary, and tomorrow will be better and the day after that better still. Economy when you are young is a game. In some circumstances it can even be fun.

I seemed to be the only passenger over thirty on the plane, which, due to mechanical difficulties that did not reassure, would not take off until 3:30 A.M. Everybody but me shrugged, opened ham sandwiches and a beer, lay down on the floor with their heads in someone's lap and fell asleep. I was the last living grown-up in the world, Anna deplaning for Siam, sitting bolt upright in my chair, vigilant eye on my carryon luggage.

But they were there at the barrier to meet me when I arrived, and it was light and I felt better. Ian looked nervous, a bit scruffy and anxious to please. They would take me to this nice hotel, well, really a bed and breakfast they had found quite near their flat. So conveniently close. Joan, looking proud and confident, led the way, she the parent and I the child, having explained to me the mysteries of the metro and the franc.

We traveled for hours, first by metro and later, when I

got reckless, by taxi. As the meter clicked merrily away, the neighborhood turned increasingly down at the heel, trash cans appeared at the curbs, small groups of loitering young men stared at us negligently as we passed. At last the driver drew uncertainly to a halt in front of a row of disreputable-looking flats, rolled down the window to peer myopically out to check the number, pushed back his cap and shouted, "Voilà."

A small hush fell over the backseat as I extricated my feet from the baggage to take a look around. Inside it was even worse than I feared. An unusually dirty man with a toothpick in his mouth lounged behind the desk, staring silently at me.

I returned to the cab and got back in.

"Did you see this place before you booked me into it?" I demanded sternly of Joan.

She nodded, looking suddenly very young.

"I paid in advance," she quavered. "I had to borrow some from Ian."

I was relentless.

"If you saw it before," I said, looking her dead in the eye, "there is no excuse for you thinking I could stay here."

"But we're poor," she said and burst into tears.

I put my arms around her, and the driver, unnerved by this scene straight out of Dickens or whatever the French equivalent is, killed the motor and began to cluck. His knowledge of English was obviously rudimentary but he understood tears, and in the back seat of his taxi they distressed him. In a torrent of voluble Gallic sympathy of which I understood about half, he informed us that he knew a nice, clean, cheap hotel. Would madame . . . ? Madame would, I said, drying everybody's tears. We left the man with the toothpick behind.

We drove sniveling to the hotel, where it was love at

first sight. It had, it is true, no telephones, no porters and my room was on the fifth floor. The bath was around the corner, and the floor of my room slanted away from the window so sharply that the bureau had been wedged in place with a wooden block. The whole hotel seemed to lean away from the street as if not sure it wanted to be associated with it, and there was no light except on the ceiling. I liked it. It was decent and respectable, a dowager hotel that had known better days, like me. I hauled my bags into the rickety elevator, accepted a key to the front door, patted the hotel cat and felt at home.

Evenings Ian showed Joan and me a Paris I could never have imagined. He was one of those Americans who have been brought up in the capitals of Europe by State Department parents and his French was impeccable. He knew the city like a Frenchman and he took us places I never expected to be. In one particularly smoky, noisy, boîte, where professional jazz musicians met to jam, my head began to ache and I recklessly decided to go back to the hotel alone. Outside the door I quailed at what I had undertaken, but there was no turning back and I hurried along the narrow street, praying for a taxi and deliverance from footpads. When an ancient rattly conveyance finally hove into sight I fell into its back seat with the kind of relief condemned prisoners must experience opening their pardons from the governor.

On two evenings the young mumbled apologetically of other engagements. On the second, thinking of Alexia, I took a luxuriant bath in the hotel's common bathtub, got into one of my better dresses and summoned a taxi to take me to one of the plush hotels which I knew cater to American tourists.

"Madame is alone?" inquired the waiter, bowing.

"Madame is alone," I agreed, trying not to think in how many ways.

He led me to a nice table where, fortified with cocktails, I ate a delicious, solitary and very expensive dinner and fled only just before the roaming gypsy string trio reached my table. They were cueing their songs to the patrons, working their way across the room with their ancient American repertoire—"Tea for Two" for the young couple by the window, "Juanita" for the Spanish group near the front, "Thank Heaven for Little Girls" for the family with the two little daughters swinging their legs and giggling in the limelight.

What would they have played for me?

Chapter 6

THE ONLY thing I learned in Paris was that whatever problems you run from will await your return. The house seemed even more empty without Joan, the bank account even more depleted—which it was. I felt enormously depressed, especially when I discovered that, by being very very careful, I had spent in Paris just fifty dollars more than the bill the dogs had managed to run up at their posh kennel. Each had had a room with a view and a bath (required), but there had been a fifty-cent charge each time Frieda had to have a pill or an eyedrop. I had especially left her geriatric vitamins at home for this reason, but I was smitten with remorse when I saw her, so ancient and feeble and shrunk up. If she hadn't cried for joy all the way home, her old gray muzzle pointed up in the air like a coyote's, I might have felt I was making a mistake trying to keep her alive by sheer determination.

It was now four months since Booth had died, and I seemed to be making progress backward. For three days in a row I woke up crying, which shocked and scared me because I couldn't connect it with any particular difficulty. Tears on the pillow so early in the morning embarrassed me, and I refused to give in to them. I got up, put on my makeup with special care and went down to see a placement bureau advertising itself as being in touch with opportunities for women starting again in mid-life.

The young woman who interviewed me had hair down to her beltline and looked as if she knew she would never have to wait her turn like me for an employment opportunity. She would have handled things better.

"Just take this over to the desk there," she said in a well-bred voice, "and write your resumé."

I wrote it, but there were terrible gaps when I was engaged in changing diapers, running car pools, being a cub-scout mother. She looked at it a while, pushing back her hair with a pencil, and eyed me thoughtfully.

"You were a reporter?" she said, obviously not believing it. "Are you looking for a reporter job now?"

Well, no, I didn't suppose so. There were those gaps, undeniably. Somebody would be sure to say things had changed.

Well, what then?

Something, perhaps, in the field? Something suitable for paying the gas bill?

She pursed her lips, looking especially fetching. My resumé was not done in the approved way. The approved way is to list the last job first. But really there was no last job.

I got up.

"Well, try," I said. "Anything, really."

I was halfway out the door when a thought struck me and I turned round.

"Anything but baby-sitting," I said and closed the door.

The woman I was looking at in the bathroom mirror every morning didn't look good. Lines had appeared where no lines had been before, the eyes seemed to be suspended in hammocks and she looked as if she didn't care. Staring at the mirror thoughtfully as I brushed my teeth, I wondered why a Higher Power had arranged it so that age in men hints of strength, things learned and sexual prowess, while in women it merely makes us look used. No wonder we have to employ every artifice available in the ads. Another inequality that should be getting more attention from the activists. The young woman at the employment agency didn't know about the bathroom mirror in her future. But then, of course, she would undoubtedly raise a family and keep her job at the same time and never have to fill out resumés wrong in her fifties, trying to cover up decades of being a housewife. She would retire on a good pension and, through years of jogging, have retained both her looks and her stamina.

Across the city blocks between us, I wished her bad cess.

"How was Paris?" inquired Alexia, but the trip had already faded in my mind like a distant dream. Coming back to the empty house had finally brought it home to me that this was the way it was going to be. This was my future.

Sundays were the worst. Sundays my friends were incommunicado, turned inward toward families. Each Sunday I read the funny papers in careful detail, took a swim and a long walk with Katie, ate a peanut-butter sandwich and tried to figure what to do with the rest of the day. I became a Sunday matinee movie fan, especially on three-day weekends. They were a necklace of terrible Sundays strung together.

"You mustn't join the widows' club," said Booth when he knew he was going to die and I was still refusing to believe it. I brushed it away then. He wasn't going to die. I wouldn't let him. Now, over the weekends, I wondered what other widows did.

Maybe the fault was mine. I must be scintillating, ask people in in droves, do more than my share of entertaining. I began a program of small dinners, one every two weeks. Every two weeks I stood on tiptoe on the kitchen stool and got down the best dishes and wineglasses, spent a whole day cooking up something that didn't need me in the kitchen at the last moment. Nothing was too much trouble—shine the silver, wear your best dress so that there could be no lingering hint that this is a second-class evening, light the candles, get plenty of ice out early. Pretend it's almost the same.

It was Katie who enjoyed these evenings. Anchored by her leash to the piano leg, pawing the air in her frustrated attempt to hurl herself at the guests, she longed to wade into the parties. If I left her too long tethered, she simply chewed through the leash and joined the guests, brought her well-mouthed treasures and laid them in their laps, trotting from one to another like a pony in the house. Universally they were repelled. The dog I got to keep me from being lonesome was driving my friends away.

The bar in the living room, chocolate mousse in the tray, the wine breathing on the kitchen table—see, I can do it alone. I can do it without him even though his going nearly destroyed me. Don't mind my dog, keep me in your life.

The guests came and went home. But I saw them elsewhere mostly at cocktail parties.

"How long have you been a widow?" asked the man standing next to me at some sort of buffet.

How did he know I was a widow? Was it the most significant fact about me that a mutual acquaintance had mentioned? Did it show like a visible scar?

"Almost five months," I told him and was struck by the echoes of childhood. "How old are you?" one asks a young child, and he replies proudly, "I'll be three in August." I could hear myself saying, "He died a year ago next March." I shivered a little and drained the glass.

He looked at me curiously.

"It must be difficult," he said, and I nodded, lump back in my throat.

I was walking a narrow ledge, walking carefully so I needn't look down to see there was no net, nobody there at all to catch me if I fell. Keep doing the next thing, one foot in front of the other, a high-wire balancing act, am I hungry? am I tired? The rest is not to be thought about.

But my mind, which was operating so dully on nearly everything, was an artist at painting finely detailed pictures of disaster. I knew I too would die of cancer and soon, the children bending low over my bed straining to catch my last words whispered through parched lips. Every twinge of my body presaged the moment when the doctor would look at me and say, "I'm sorry, it seems so incredible that you could develop the same disease as your husband. But I'm afraid you have only at best a year."

I sat in the doctor's waiting room despairing, but when the examination was over he patted me on the head and said I was fine, just fine. I had rarely been less fine, but I did allow him to convince me that I was not dying of cancer. I went home relieved but still low in my mind.

"I'm worried about you," murmured my friend, Ruth. "You seem somehow to have been doing better earlier."

"I don't know," I said, the lump returning in my throat at the slightest hint of sympathy. "I seem always to be on the verge of tears."

"I'm taking you to Emilio's for lunch," she said briskly, her voice gathering me up like a cheerful nanny who knows best. "Meet me at twelve."

Ruth is very generous and understands the basic fact that any problem, no matter how insoluble, is improved by a new dress or a nice lunch at a posh place.

The head waiter bowed low—Ruth's husband is very important—and led us to a table near the window. Very expensive and delicious dishes were proferred in succession, solicitous attention was lavished. Muscles I hadn't known were tied into knots untied, fears I hadn't admitted receded before the smell of comforting luxury. I sipped my coffee and felt better.

Ruth took out her compact and powdered her nose.

"Are you getting plenty of sleep?" she said, tucking it back in her bag.

Dear Ruth, enveloped in a large, devoted family and financial security beyond the possibility of reverses, is apt to equate sensible living with the solutions to life's pain. Illness is the one thing that could possibly intrude into her life's charmed circle, and sleep wards off illness. One must be vigilant, take care of one's self and sometimes of one's friends.

I sighed.
"More than I need, probably," I told her.
"You don't want to get sick," she said.
"No," I agreed.
"Well," she said, giving me a sunny smile, "you know Bill and I are fond of you, and you must take care of yourself." She reached for the check, shrugging off nonpositive thoughts, and I was afraid for a moment she might remind me that a proper lady keeps a cheerful face. But she only pocketed the change and gathered up her gloves. "I must fly," she said apologetically. "A meeting." Making a little moue.
"Right," I said, "and thanks."
All the way home the lunch sat like a stone in my stomach.

Katie's nose was at the door, and I sat on the floor to put my arms around her. Everybody needs love, and when two-legged love is beyond your reach, four-legged love is the next-best thing. It shouldn't be inferred from this, of course, that I have ever considered dog love second class. Count me among those who, standing at the pearly gates with my ID stamped, will shake my head and say, uh uh, not without my dog. I am very sorry for anyone who has never been loved by a dog.

Frieda was now lost in the dream world of the elderly, sleeping her life away on the hall rug, but Katie and I were indivisible. In my bath she loomed over me, dropping in her toys one by one. In the car she sat erect and vigilant beside me, searching the bus stops ever hopefully for Joan. Nights she snuggled up to my slippers beside the bed, and if I woke to turn over, I automatically activated her tail.

I was not oblivious to the fact that many people do not feel this way about dogs. Dogs, they will say carefully, are all right in their place. Katie definitely has never known her place, and future hope for this is dim. Frieda is a household fixture, above discipline and deferred to. The best patches of sun are hers. That kind of thing is understood and accepted. I bend to their peculiarities and perquisites as I would to those of old friends, but not everybody was prepared to join me in this.

I was giving a party and had just led the guests into the dining room, pointed out their chairs and disappeared for that last zero moment of dishing out what was to be eaten. While scooping out the curry, I heard one of the guests call to me that Frieda was sleeping behind her chair and preventing it being pulled out. Proper seating had ground to a halt.

Where Frieda chose to nap at the particular moment was a matter of absolutely no interest to me. I was as engrossed as a surgeon lifting his scalpel, and I called back to take my chair and I would arrange things later. I went on scooping out curry, sprinkling raisin and coconut and ground pickle and, at last ready, I was bearing the steaming platter to the table when I encountered a male guest leading Frieda by the collar from the room.

Everything inside me froze like a game of still pond, no moving. My ancient dowager dog was being ousted, half-led, half-assisted from her chosen place. What kind of liberties were being taken? Not to put too fine a point on it, how dare he?

I clutched at the remnants of hospitality, donning a false smile.

"Where are you going with my poor old dog?" I inquired through my teeth.

"Well, Mary doesn't like . . ." he began, but I had already heard enough. Anger swept over me like a brush fire. I plunked the curry on the table, scooped Frieda up in my arms and thrust her out into the backyard, slammed the door on her and, slipping graciously into my place, surveyed the ruins of my dinner party in furious silence. In some obscure way they had overstepped the boundaries, made free with arrangements not the prerogatives of guests. I was locked into frozen disapproval, from which there was no retreat. I sat like a vengeful Buddha, unable to eat, as the nervous conversation swirled around me.

If the picture of a grown woman sitting in injured silence in her own house because a guest has taken liberties with her dog provokes a smile, I can only say I agree. I was a bystander and a principal performer both, and I only report what happened. There was no logic to it. I wasn't in control. I was a package of raw emotions tied together with loose string that had just come unraveled. It wasn't until long afterward that I understood how hard we survivors are to deal with.

Rain or shine, I walked the dogs, the same walk every morning, sweet routine. Frieda was part of a happier life, the link with how it used to be, and I had some dim idea that when she was gone, so would be a piece of the old life. Daily we made our solemn, measured progress around the neighborhood, investigating every tree and bush, lingering to read the messages left by previous dogs. Two blocks up, cross the street, two blocks back. I scheduled my life around when she had to be let out or walked. And then one morning she appeared to be tripping over something that wasn't there.

I took her in my arms, an ancient dog already deaf and now unable to see at all, and went straight to the vet. He shook his head, but I couldn't accept it. I carried her home, dropping tears on her head, and sought out a dog ophthalmologist I had heard of.

Ushered into his office, holding her close, I quavered my doubts. She would never see again, would she? Some of my friends thought that perhaps it was time to pull the plug. Some of my friends, I said, choking on the words, thought I was being absurd about a dog. She was, after all, eighteen, and a good pat could knock her over. Only see how frail she is.

The doctor was a slender man with a Freudian beard and a clipped manner. He listened carefully, leaned forward on his elbows, weight on the desk between us, and fixed me with a penetrating eye.

"Fuck 'em," he said, and I knew I had found the right man.

He could not make her see again, but he could take the pain away. Yes, there was pain. Glaucoma and now slipped lenses in both eyes. They were rolled up like those of a knocked-out prizefighter in the comic strips. He wrote prescriptions busily. Pills three times a day, drops in each eye twice a day, all presented to the pharmacist in my drugstore with her name on them. The first batch was twenty-seven dollars. I flinched visibly and demanded a senior-citizen discount, but he looked at me stonily and said it didn't matter how old the dog was, it didn't count.

At the parties now, the guests had to be careful not to step on her.

Chapter 7

I WAS reading a letter from Joan when the telephone rang. I had just gotten, for the second time, to the part about she and Ian hitchhiking to Chartres and how there was really no danger in bumming a ride over there, it was only in the States. She had bought a skirt in a flea market, there was a fabulous exhibit of watercolors at a little gallery, and again the telephone intruded.

"This is Alexia Campbell's neighbor," said the stranger's voice. "She has asked me to tell you that Mr. Campbell was taken ill last night and she is with him now at the hospital."

Sick in the night? Why wasn't Alexia calling herself? A weak sensation settled around my knees, and I replaced the receiver with both hands as if it were very fragile. I had had dinner with George and Alexia only two nights before. Viral pneumonia, perhaps, a sudden high temperature? Appendicitis? Why had I put down the telephone without asking what the trouble was? I reached for my coat with a shaking hand.

I recognized Alexia's back from the full length of the corridor, ramrod straight, strong. She was talking with two men in white coats, and one was shaking his head. I waited in the distance until the conversation should be over. Nothing good was being said. I could not see her face, only the faces of the men, but I could read the news from the way all three stood. All of it was bad.

They turned away, turned back to add something, and then Alexia was coming toward me down the corridor, walking carefully as if it were narrow and dangerous, beset by hidden dragons.

When she spoke, it was as if she were continuing a conversation, as if we had been talking all along.

"George is so young," she said, and her voice was very insistent to make me understand. "I told them he was young, and they thought I was talking about them. 'George is young,' I said. 'You are babies. George is only sixty-one.'"

"Let's go get some coffee," I said.

It was heart, and George did not last the day. They pulled out all the tubes and pulled a sheet over his face, and I wasn't even with her. I only found out when I called that afternoon to suggest she have dinner with me and she said she didn't think she could, George was dead.

I went around and sat on her sofa as if I were company, and I had learned a lot, so I knew what to say.

"Tell me how he died," I commanded.

She told me everything in that strange, detached manner that we widows slip into, and I could hear myself those few months ago, telling someone on the phone whom I didn't even know very well, "He died in my arms in the kitchen." Someone has to ask this, maybe an old friend, maybe a curiosity seeker. You cannot distinguish very well at the time between them, but it doesn't matter much. The important thing is to tell someone how it was.

It was very hot the day of the funeral, the last gasp of a cruel Indian summer. I sat in the pew a few seats back from Alexia and wept openly, tears streaming down my face as she sat dry-eyed between her children, giving the minister courteous attention. I was not weeping especially for George, gone beyond tears, but for myself and for Booth and for Alexia and for all of us, the ones left behind and the ones who leave. The last torrid sultriness of the summer's heat crept in the open door into the church, and I picked up the fan on the seat beside me more to hide behind than to stir up an air current. "Adams & Son, Undertakers," it said on the palm fronds.

Outside the church Alexia turned and shook the hand of every guest. When it was my turn, tears still wet on my face, the new widow looked at me with genuine sympathy.

"You mustn't cry," she said. "He wouldn't want you to."

Her turn to weep would come later.

"You look so thin," I said to her a week or two later over the crepes in our restaurant.

She made a little impatient gesture.

"It gets stuck here," she said, hand on her throat. "I go to a restaurant and they put it in front of me and I can't get it down." She smiled deprecatingly, to show that it wasn't really important, just an interesting anatomical phenomenon. "And at home it isn't worthwhile for just me."

"You must eat," I said sternly, mother to child, old girl to new girl. "Every day, three decent meals. It's important."

She toyed with her crepe, turning it over and staring at it absently.

"Alexia, dear Alexia, are you getting along all right?"

"Pretty well," she said.

It is very hard to tell from looking at Alexia what she is thinking. I long to say, "Complain, cry, lean on me and say you find the house frighteningly empty, full of shadows. I, after all, know the territory, of all people can understand." But if I did, she would only smile and say other people are too busy to hear her troubles, and if I inquired what friends are for, she would brush that off too. Forget this scenario. Alexia bites the silver bullet, and never more than after George's death.

We ate a bit in silence, and then she put down her fork.

"If only," she said, and for the first time I saw something slip through the control, "I had someone to tell it to."

If only. It is perhaps the worst deprivation of all. Terrible things, funny things, strange things happen to you all day, and you want to save them up to tell to somebody. For a whole week, in that strange dreamlike aftermath of Booth's death, I wrote down things I would have told him, as if he were just away and we would catch up later, and I mustn't forget to tell him. I have no idea what I thought I was doing. It was simply that those things had to be collected somewhere besides inside my head. Things like the fact that they were building on the vacant lot where the wild asters grew. Or that I had seen a cat run over, squashed flat in the rear and the front part still trying to get up. I wanted somebody to say how awful for me, what was I planning for dinner, overlay it all with a sense of the world going along in spite of this. I told the dogs. When you are talking to dogs, it doesn't count as talking to yourself.

"I know you know about that," said Alexia.

"But you have me," I pointed out.

"You're busy too," said Alexia.

"I wish I were."

It was her turn to be solicitous.

"Any luck at all?"

I shook my head.

"I'm looking for an elderly pensioner not long for this world. I will be very nice to him for a few months and then I will slip a little something in his tea.

"I am about ready," I said, "to marry for money. Any candidates?"

She wasn't sure I was joking, and neither was I.

"I don't know any unmarried men," she said.

"At least you're solvent," I said, and I heard the twinge of bitterness in my voice.

"Yes," she said, "but I'm going to sell the house."

Sell the house? I stared at her. I couldn't believe she'd said it.

"A smaller place," she said. "Too full of memories."

I opened my mouth, recollected just in time that the house was hers not mine, no matter how I counted on it being there.

"A house you've lived in ten years? You're going to go through and toss things, give them away, sell them?"

"Yes."

"The books and the three sets of silver and the letters from George when he was in the war and the photograph albums? You're going to go through all those and pack them up to move?"

"Yes," she said. "I don't want to live there anymore."

"Listen," I said, "there's this society in town that sends people out to call on new widows so they can ask questions and discuss what to do and what not to do. They say you shouldn't make any big step for a year."

She was going to leave behind the weeping willow we had sat under, the rambler rose from which George cut his boutonniere every day in the summer. She was toying with my memories.

"You're determined?" I said, and it wasn't really a question.

She nodded.

She did what she said she was going to do. A large For Sale sign went up that meant another corner of my familiar world was going to be removed. But I seemed to have turned some kind of personal corner, and what should have pushed me further into despondency somehow didn't upset my equilibrium as I thought it would. Something had pulled me out of my funk; possibly thinking about somebody else for a change. Once more I was getting up in the morning thinking life was possible. Once more I began to enjoy the smell of the morning coffee, the sight of the chickadee at the bird feeder, the new sharp smell of the coming autumn. And then, suddenly, almost as a reward, I got a job.

A lot of things about that job are etched forever in my mind, but not exactly how I got it. I know that Chris, who had lived next door but one, got it for me, but what I said to bring it about is gone forever. I only remember Chris standing in my living room, languid and self-assured with twenty-three years of living, wearing tight jeans and cowboy boots and asking if I'd be interested in doing some advertising writing. I remember saying I'd be interested in anything, and he nodded and went off bearing whatever thing he had come to borrow or leaving behind what he had returned. I didn't think much about it, really.

I should have. Chris is the kind of young man who does what he sets out to do. It is almost frightening how success and positive vibes radiate from Chris. He managed to get accepted at every college to which he applied and went to two or three of them, I forget how many, because Chris is always moving on to something better. The sight of him has caused more than one prospective employer to change his job requirements, and it is hard to believe that he will ever encounter failure. He did everything first and better than anyone—he even got married when everybody else just had living arrangements. It is whispered, I am told, that he is secretly shy, but it must be the best-kept secret within a hundred miles. From out front he looks like the granddaddy of all self-assurance.

The reason I didn't take him seriously is that he was always underfoot when Joan was growing up. He came to dinner and ate his first artichoke at our house, learned to ride a bicycle in our backyard. He grew very gradually into a tall, lean-hipped young man with black blown-dry hair, while he was frozen in time in my mind looking respectfully up at me while I explained about life.

But a man from the advertising agency called the next morning and seemed to feel that if Chris said I would do, I would do. I went into town to see him, clutching my list of credits nervously, but he had obviously already decided. They showed me to a cubicle with an IBM Selectric, told me I would be doing some brochure work on a refrigerator account, gave me a sheaf of booklets and told me to go to it.

Chris was down the hall somewhere in a private glass office with a view and waved in friendly fashion when passing. In the cubicles adjoining mine everybody was very young, laid back and friendly, fond of yogurt and Pepsi, and had shining hair. I kept wondering how it was that they had had time to become so obviously competent, so confident that they could handle what was required, when I, who had been reporting and writing before they were born, was so uneasy.

Three days a week and near enough for me to rush home and let the dogs out at noon. I could write a lot and garner enough money to stop worrying. I could stock the kitchen shelves with tuna against the next moneyless time, buy the car a new dependable battery, stop having nightmares about the tax clerk. Suddenly I was once more a dues-paying member of society, part of the working world, solvent and a commuter.

The only trouble was I couldn't figure out how to run the typewriter.

While I had been raising the children, something had happened to typewriters. At our house typewriters had never been plugged in, never sat humming in impatience if thoughts did not flow swiftly. A firm touch such as my little manual Olympia required sent the carriage of this typewriter skittering in panic. Mysterious buttons ruled the tabs, turned the whole contraption on and off. When I went home at night, I was sure I had forgotten to turn it off, that it would develop a life of its own and gradually become red hot, setting the place afire like a stove left on. I decided to deny everything and claim a mouse chewed the insulation.

My fellow workers put graphics designers and printers on hold and tried to teach me to trust it. Not by a flicker of an eyelash did they imply that many people consider electric typewriters standard equipment. I listened attentively, did as I was told, and after two days toted into the city my own machine and hid the electric under the desk. Nights I thought about the Olympia all alone in that deep-carpeted, plant-studded jungle. It looked like a second-hand Ford that had blundered by mistake into a Cadillac showroom.

"Getting along all right?" said the Head, passing among her troops, lacquer haired, clunky shoed and gimlet eyed. The agency was her baby.

"Just fine," I replied brightly, smiling up at her falsely, and she moved on.

Here, Head, take my hand, we're going back a bit. I want you to meet my first boss, right here wearing the green eyeshade, the one with the cigar dangling from the corner of his mouth like Ned Sparks. Maybe you don't remember Ned Sparks? Mind where you step, it gets a little damp in this basement office when it rains. It seeps under the door from the street above. That's my typewriter over there, that Remington standard, very noisy and the *e* key sticks. There's just the two of us in this branch office, and when things get dull he whacks his desk with his crutch and yells, "Christ Almighty, it's as quiet as a whorehouse on Sunday afternoon. We got to stir up something."

Say howdy, Head. This is a very nice man.

The light on my telephone blinked, and I jumped and picked it up.

"Conley Associates," I said into the receiver, but the other light was blinking, too.

If only I could figure out how to put somebody on hold.

Chapter 8

"You look different," said Alexia as we sat toasting ourselves in front of her fire. "Being employed has made a difference."

I thought about it.

"So much refrigeration shrivels the soul," I told her, "but there is hardly anything in life that isn't a little easier to bear if you have enough money."

She didn't look as if she believed it. I could see her thinking that she had enough money and nothing was easier to bear. She seemed to have shrunk up somehow, as if a strong wind would blow her away like a leaf.

She saw me looking at her and smiled.

"I think it gets easier later," I said. "I read it somewhere."

"Don't tell me how I'm supposed to feel," she said,

sitting up a little straighter. "I refuse to be programmed." She got to her knees and stirred the fire thoughtfully, a woman no longer young but handsome. "Have you noticed," she said as she put the poker back in its stand, "that the world is being run by kids these days? The policemen, the lawyers, especially the doctors. Where are the authoritative father figures? I feel old."

That's Alexia. Get close to the bone and she slips away like a trout you try to catch with your bare hands. But maybe she was right and I was wrong, and if you never mention pain, paint it over with shellac and pretend it's not there, it doesn't exist. I don't believe it for a minute.

"Constantly," I said. "Everybody is thirty, a young professional with blow-dried hair. I'm terribly afraid they'll notice me and I'll be left out to die on an ice floe. So far they haven't mentioned it, but they're only being polite."

"How did it get to be such a disgrace?" murmured Alexia, mostly to herself. "Somebody about sixteen gave me the finger yesterday because I didn't realize I should turn right on red."

She put down her dessert plate untouched on the hearth and locked her arms around her knees.

"We're outnumbered," I said, "and we did it. It's the wartime baby boom. Eat up all your nice chocolate cake."

Christmas, if you're alone, is Sunday to the nth power, and all the holes in the life you put together for yourself become glaringly apparent. The papers are always full of people who realize on Christmas that it isn't worthwhile going on alone. Christmas by yourself would be even worse than your birthday alone, because the rules say at

Christmas *everybody* has to be happy. Children may have been invented to come home at Christmas and take care of this lost feeling.

Mine were coming. Both of them. With my new financial resources, I had cabled the money to Joan along with a message saying, "Come home for Christmas. He has you the rest of year." She said she would.

We were planning to give as usual the Christmas Eve open house, but the thought of filling that champagne punch bowl and stuffing those stockings by myself panicked me again. I stayed extra hours at Conley Associates, trying to produce more words. But try as I would, some things remained forever incomprehensible to me. The politics behind it all were baffling; the flacks of some companies, it seemed, were to be trusted, whereas . . . but what is a flack? When I had to ask, I knew it was a black mark. People who don't know that flacks are public-relations counsels are noticeably over thirty. It seems I had been married to a flack for more than thirty years but neither of us knew it. I had revealed a basic gap, though everybody was too polite to mention it.

Chris I saw occasionally in the hall and through the window of his new glassed-in private office. He looked abstracted and competent. I told him I thought I could handle the job, and he seemed genuinely pleased. At morning meetings presided over by the Head, I watched him carefully. He didn't look worried. He obviously did not suffer the cold feeling in the gut when the Head dissected story by story the work we had done. He looked reliable and relaxed. One of my efforts was favorably commented on, but the Head was mercurial, difficult to please and remote. I waited nervously for my first misstep and tried to avoid meeting her in the hall. I loved being solvent.

I was bound by a common lack of esprit de corps to the other occupants of the cubicles. We had the camaraderie of Foreign Legionnaires waiting out a hitch. All of us planned to move on when we could, needed the job for the moment. We shared gossip, rumors, the names of sources and opinions and bad jokes on the behavior and private life of the Head. A notice appeared on the bulletin board offering free stress tabs to all staff members. I felt it was a bad omen, but the checks kept coming in, and each week the threat of poverty receded a bit more into the distance. I learned to call flacks and minor officials Slick and Badger and inquire after their love lives. The world seemed a little more possible.

We were all invited to attend the Christmas party of Conley Associates at the home of the Head.

"Will you be bringing anybody?" inquired her secretary, checking my name off on her list, but I shook my head.

When the evening arrived, I knew myself for the impostor I was. Minus my typewriter and my phone with flashing lights, I seemed to be alien, to have no reason to be there. What was I doing all dressed up in my best dress at an office party? I caught a glimpse of Chris, leaning negligently against the staircase, his arm around the shoulders of a girl whose long hair glinted in the candlelight. I felt de trop and and passed on, waving jauntily. All my small talk, unless about my brochure, was unsuitable. I felt like an aging Cinderella without proper instructions from my grandmother.

"Be sure," whispered one of my new friends from the next cubicle, "to say thanks to Harold before you leave."

"Harold?" I repeated stupidly.

She made an engaging little gesture that explained everything and nothing. "Very important," she said. "Check in."

Harold was very gracious when I said I'd had a lovely time.

Alexia was right, the job made a difference, not only in my escape from bankruptcy but in my self-esteem. I liked myself a lot better, I was making new friends, I had this nice job where they seemed to like me. The checks were fatter and fatter, and I breathed a little easier. I found a car pool with a friend, learned the train schedule for when she had to work late, and felt the direction of everything was up.

It took a lot out of me. The pressure built all week, and deadlines, after more than thirty years, made me nervous. Nights when I put my key in the lock and the dogs got up stretching to meet me, I knew more about Booth than I had ever known. I was too tired to do anything but read the paper and eat my dinner, and I remembered, wincing, laying the problems of the day on him while he washed his hands tiredly after the commuter train. Home, I discovered, is not only where they have to take you in but where you are safe from being held accountable for anything that goes wrong. The girl who quit her job in 1946 was fading out of focus. The problems of domesticity had been demoted, and I had crossed over from the passenger side.

To the friends of my former existence, I had entered a foreign country. I was still seeing them for card games on my days off, but the three days I spent in my cubicle were outside their sphere of interest. If one of my children had fallen ill, every detail would have been demanded of me; if I had decided to move from my house, every eye would have sparkled with interest. Maybe you have to be able to identify, to imagine that this can happen to you. Nobody I knew in my Before could ever imagine finding herself in Conley Associates.

At first they met me for lunch, complaining that it was difficult to find my office. After a while they ceased to come. I ate a lot of yogurt in the park with my new friends.

Chris quit Conley Associates for a better job, and the rest of us were all admiring. The Head was loathe to let him go, was rumored to have offered him more money, but he shook his black hair and said the new job would be more meaningful. It was close by, he told me, and we could lunch occasionally. I took him for a farewell feast at an expensive restaurant nearby, and he quizzed me for the last time about the way to get ahead in journalism. I really hated to see him go.

After five I was still lonely, so I decided to give a party for my co-workers. It was a huge success, everybody agreed, and it must have been, because nobody went home till three, at which point I could barely drag myself upstairs. I made a mental note to explain to Alexia that the young run the world because they have more stamina. When I fell asleep I dreamed of George, lying in his hospital bed with Alexia standing over him murmuring, "George is so young."

In the night I woke several times and dreamed fitfully, this time of my father, a widower for twenty years. Young, I might as well have tried to imagine how it was to be the spaniel lying in front of the fire as to imagine what problems he suffered. When he told me he didn't feel old, I felt uneasy. He was old, I could see that; he was already forty-five. When he gave his endless parties, when he went to get his shoes shined or his hair cut of an evening, I never understood why. Parents don't get lonely. Then he went and died before I understood and could ask him what he had learned along the way.

Everybody but me got a week off with pay at Christmas at Conley Associates, but I got the week off. I met Joan at the plane and Katie went wild, hurling herself into her lap, burrowing her nose into her neck, kissing her face. The next plane brought Ted from Boston and the family circle was as complete as we could make it. We hung the wreaths, bought the tree, picked the best Christmas cards for posting on a red felt roll of honor, tied red ribbons on the necks of the dogs.

I wanted to ask Joan how it was in Paris, but every time I opened my mouth, the words got stuck. I kept talking around what I wanted desperately to know.

"Do you lunch at the Ritz much?" I began. It was, I could see the moment I got it out, a bit heavyhanded to pass as banter, but I wanted to make her smile.

Did I imagine it or did she look different? More, well . . . self-assured. She seemed to have slipped so easily into the expatriate life that I felt depressed. She was going to embrace it and France, leaving three thousand miles of ocean between us.

She was looking at me tolerantly.

"Do you think Ian and I are bloated capitalists?" she said and that was all I learned from that. Imagination is a curse.

Alexia was going to spend the holidays with her married daughter in Chicago, in a big house with lots of dogs and children in the suburbs. I had a moment's cold-flash vision of me reduced to visiting Joan over the holidays in her walk-up, a package of the Head's stress pills in my purse. A cheap hotel on Christmas morning and a jolly Christmas dinner at a cheap Chinese restaurant.

We did the Christmas party the way we always had, everything as much as possible the same. All our friends made a special effort to come, though on Christmas Eve it is so inviting to stay home. Even Chris came, announcing that he was very happy in his new office. I didn't invite my new friends. I seemed to have a foot in two vastly different worlds, and I wasn't sure the inhabitants of each would understand the other. We filled the punch bowl with cheap champagne and white wine, put out the fruitcake and pretended everything was all right.

They all came, the couples we had known when I was part of a pair, their children whom Ted and Joan had grown up with. Somebody had sleigh bells around his neck as usual, somebody brought an enormous, revolting-looking Santa Claus, everybody got a little drunk, slipped arms around me and admired the hors d'oeuvres. The room was bulging with people, laughing and kissing and trying to find a place to put their empty glasses and their ashes, and I felt I had done something vastly important, vaulted some hurdle I had dreaded. Then they were streaming out the door in a wash of frigid air and it was all over. It had gone well.

We didn't clean up right away. We just cleared a place in the living room and stared at the fire and rested our feet, promising ourselves to open a can of soup when we felt stronger.

"It's a good kind of party," said Ted. "We should keep giving it, every year, year after year, the way we always have."

"Of course," I said, staring at the fire. "That's understood."

It had never occurred to me to do otherwise. Never have I been the one to let a flagging friendship die with an unanswered letter, never the first to cross an acquaintance who is becoming a dim face from a Christmas-card list. I like things to go comfortingly on the way they always have, and whatever I can do to ensure it, I do. No dog goes out of my life until the last possible breath, no car leaves me to make way for a shiny new replacement without a pang. I get used to things, to people. Some might call it not knowing when to quit.

It went well, we all said again, inspecting the dying logs in the fireplace, thinking our own thoughts with our shoes off. For one more December they had come home to make the house bloom with their youth and nose-thumbing confidence in themselves and the future. I hadn't been alone at all, I had gotten through it and maybe I could handle the Christmases that would come after.

Ted rose and kicked the logs and, watching his turned back, I reflected on the perversity of genes, which make of your children reflections of people you scarcely know. I replayed the party, watching him introduce people, making them laugh, replenishing the punch bowl as he had watched his father do so long, playing host.

And then I sat up very straight.

"How did you do it?" I demanded. "How did you know how to make your father's Christmas punch?"

He began to gather up empty punch glasses, dump cigarette butts and scrabbled-up paper napkins into the fire.

"He gave me the recipe last year," he said. "And he told me, 'Take care of your mother; I won't be here next year.'"

Chapter 9

"Fourteen years," says my hairdresser, her lips compressed with anger. "Fourteen years I was alone—nobody cared." She backcombs my hair so fiercely that tears of pain start to my eyes. "Now I am married again, they come."
"Why didn't they come when you were widow?" I ask. I have a tendency to drop my articles the way she does when I talk to her. "Was it because you hadn't had time to make friends in this country?"
"No."
The word is so clipped it could cut. She busies herself with spray, her combs, the rollers in her drawer, the tools of her trade, rearranging them on the counter. After fourteen years she is still angry. It is hard to believe so much anger is still tucked away into so small a frame.

"No," she says again. "Was because I was widow."

She holds up the mirror so I can see myself, as she once was, in it. What I am looking at is essentially what I have been seeing in this seat for years. The face is the same, but nothing else is.

"What do you eat?" my married friends asked me, leaning close to hear as they would take an interest in the strange customs of a Pacific tribe. "Lots of frozen dinners?"

Not lots of frozen dinners. Cooking, which was once a three-times-a-day bore, has now become a recreation, a delight I can amuse myself with when I want and not when I do not want. They assume cooking is for pleasing others, a chore that could be dropped if no one were there to enjoy it. On the contrary. Cooking for the first time in my life assumed new dimensions. I find it calming, reassuring, nice. When it came around three times a day regularly, I didn't care for it.

They were truly interested, giving me close attention. But I knew, before I opened my mouth, they would not want to hear the things I would say. They longed to nod approvingly over a single lamb chop with a watercress sprig, a bit of fish to keep the blood pressure from soaring, or high-class frozen dinners. Yet each of them is an excellent cook, skilled in her own kitchen.

"A roast," I told them. "I cook it on Sunday and eat it all week. Or, if I give a dinner, I eat the leftovers till they're gone."

They drew back in the face of this attack on ordered domesticity from one of their own, this deviation from accepted proper practices. And they didn't even know about the morning I had pecan pie for breakfast. My morals were dying away before my lack of obligations. I cooked when I felt in the mood, ate my dessert first if it seemed more fun that way. Who was there to please but me?

"When you entertain," asked Ruth, "isn't it a lot of work, with your job and everything?"

There's no way to explain how much work, but that's what it takes. And the old bod, as they referred to it down at Conley Associates, rebels occasionally. Sometimes, I told them, I just close the door behind the guests' retreating forms, leave the dinner table as we rose from it and go to bed.

The silence that greeted this confidence was awesome. Go upstairs without washing the dishes? Or even clearing them? A large pleasure of life, it is understood, is putting away clean dishes on the shelves after a party, stacking them neatly ready for the next time, seeing the silver back in neat, shiny rows in the sideboard, lares and penates restored to their proper places, a comfort just to gaze upon. A cardinal neglect had been uncovered. I knew. I used to feel that way, too.

"But how," persisted the gentlest of them in the tone of reproving mother to erring child, "can we come to your house when we know you let dishes sit there all night dirty?"

There I sat, the nondishwasher, an unrepentant maverick, feeling the wagons circle to protect order and domesticity. The disapproval was public censure.

I looked away, took a deep breath, but it came out anyway.

"If you're going to judge me as a housewife," I said, "I'll never make the grade."

"Listen," I said to Alexia, "I know it'll never happen to you. You never let anyone into your mind, you've got too much sense. I don't know why I can't just hold my tongue and listen. Something gets into me."

There was a soothing sound on the other end of the phone. Alexia hardly ever lays blame out loud on people, deserved or no, though privately she is obdurate.

"I long to pass the way I used to," I said. "The way you do with strangers, not rocking the boat, not telling them your opinions, just trying to be agreeable."

"That isn't friendship," she said. "Friendship is a fifty-fifty affair."

The metamorphosis of married friends into acquaintances takes time and at first is not very noticeable. At first it is a matter of the phone not ringing as often with reports on bargain shopping, requests for your lemon-pie recipe. All this was perfectably understandable since I was mostly at work, but after a while, when I noticed that my party dresses hadn't been off the hangers in months, I was frightened. Love is a gift you may or may not keep, but friendship, we are promised, endures. Did those party dresses have sisters in the closets of other single women all over town, or was I, having become too different, too thorny, the only one not seeing the insides of my friends' houses after dark? If all the couples in my life receded like an artist's rendering of perspective, what would be left to me?

I was angry, bitter and scared. Where were they all when I most needed them? Was it really possible that years of friendship can be wiped out by a change of social status? At night I had to keep my mind off the problem or sleep eluded me.

"There were times," said a stranger at the dinner table of an old friend, "when, after I was widowed, I thought I would have to talk to somebody or lose my mind."

I put my fork down and gave her my attention, lying low. No alliance with widows. It makes us into a class.

"I was in New York when it happened," she went on, sipping her wine, her eyes turning inward, "and we all know there is no lonelier place. I was fifty years old, widowed and as lonely as I ever expect to be. And you know what I did? I went to Roseland."

Well-bred incredulity hovered over our end of the table.

"I called up and asked if it was okay for somebody my age and they said, sure, everybody was welcome."

I looked at her, chic but no longer svelte—self-contained, impervious, I would have thought, to loneliness.

She was still talking. Wrong section of town, she was saying. Unknown territory. She had taken a cab, paid two dollars to get in, thinking what am I doing here? A large man with a beer belly asked her to dance and she shook her head, no thank you, and moved away. But then why had she come? Over by the refreshments, someone more possible suggested a dance and she slipped into his arms. The band was good, the place was jammed with humanity, she whirled with the unknown partner suspended from real life, and then it was time to go home. He would take her there, he said, a kiss was all he asked for the courtesy.

She fled, getting on the first bus going in the right direction. Home, when she got there, seemed cozy, sheltering, safe, no longer lonely. She had gotten through the bad time.

They listened to her story and tried to match it. A man at the end of the table had been lonely once on a foreign business trip. A woman on his left thought a psychiatrist would be a better answer, or perhaps the Y. Everyone after all has lonely moments. What lone woman would invite such dangers, such humiliations?

I kept on silently eating my beef stroganoff. Alone at that table, I knew what she was talking about.

"You expect too much of people," said Ted, suddenly turned father figure, and I nodded dumbly. The fault was mine. I accepted it. I would try harder.

I gave a large party and asked everybody who would come, swearing nobody would ever again catch me out with a controversial stand, an odd-lot opinion. I bought little dainties I couldn't afford, devoted a whole day to setting it up, put on a dress I could scarcely remember buying and a welcoming smile. Not a word, I vowed, would escape me about advertising, outlandish dietary habits, women's rights, parties I didn't attend or anything in any way basic.

I added the names of two other widows to the guest list. I had come a long way. I asked every couple I could think of, and once more the house bulged with people admiring the dip, complimenting me on my dress, asking after my children. Once more it all seemed all right; perhaps I had imagined my difficulties, taken offense where none was meant. It was after all simply a matter of pleasantries, replenishing the dip and not letting the ice run out. The only bow I made to my new life was the cheap Scotch right out on the counter.

"Can I help?"

The voice matched the face. Ruth looks the way she sounds.

"Why not?" I told her. "Dish out the salad."

She smiled that beatific smile that makes her even prettier than she is and went to work. None of Ruth's smiles is social. She never orders them up, they float to the surface, rising like cream, genuine and as uncomplicated and easygoing as her life.

"Lovely dip," she murmured, working away. "They're crazy about it."

"Good," I said. I was embroiled in what came next.

She stepped back to admire her handiwork.

"You do it all so well," she said admiringly. "And all alone. I'd be so helpless in your shoes without a husband."

"Do you ever," I asked one of my widowed guests under cover of party chat, "feel like the only grown-up in the crowd when they say they'll have to ask their husbands?"

"I don't know," she said, absently stirring her drink with a piece of ice. "I guess I just got used to it. I went to a lecture by a sociologist at the church last week, and he said widows have to change in order to survive. Maybe I'm just surviving."

"Are you sought after?" I said, smiling brilliantly to show it was a joke.

"No," she said. "I can tell when I meet my married friends that they feel guilty about me, but I don't care much anymore. Do you?"

"Yes."

She thought about it for a while.

"Last Christmas a friend of mine called and suggested I come over and help trim the tree with the children."

"You *are* sought after."

"They don't feel comfortable with us anymore," she said, and drifted off to make her way in the crowd.

I went back to work and pulled the work over my head, wrapped it around me so I didn't have any more time to think. I took Katie for long walks where she made friends with everybody we passed. I cleaned out the garage, filing the insecticides alphabetically, sweeping out the autumn leaves which were spending the winter there, storing the children's roller skates and basketballs in a box in the corner neatly. Work is a wonderful thing, even make-work.

Alexia had found a smaller house and was moving into it gradually, a load of books today, a crate of dishes tomorrow, and I was helping. She had the whole month to make the transfer and now referred to the house where she and George had spent so many years as "this old white elephant." She tossed out boxes of old letters, books inscribed to her thirty years before, old hats, gloves, pipes, divested herself of the pieces of their life together as if she were entering a nunnery.

I watched appalled. Every day a shipment of something was dispatched to one of her children.

"All the Leslie Fords?" I would quaver. "All those old political buttons that he collected for so long?"

She was adamant.

"Alice will enjoy them," she would say quietly. "There isn't much room in the new house."

I felt she was getting rid of everything I had had a part in, but I could only stagger home with some of the overflow.

"It's easier this way," she said once as we sat exhausted on the floor, surrounded by old tennis rackets and golf shoes.

I suppose we are all different. George had been dead only eight months and she seemed far more self-contained, more healed than I, who had been alone almost an entire year. I hadn't worked my way through anything. If anything, it had been growing harder lately. The balance of a life for two had shifted to just me, but I wasn't adjusted to it. Every night when I turned on the lights seemed as bad as the first.

"Why?" inquired Alexia, not mentioning how she felt when the lights went on.

"Because I thought before I could lick it. I didn't know it can get worse."

It was not long after this that I was eating dinner over the morning paper when the doorbell rang and I found an old friend on the worn doormat. I let him in, shoved the dishes to one side to make room for his cup of coffee and stared puzzled as he put into my hand a single, rather wilted yellow rose.

"For me?" I said stupidly just before I realized why he had come. Over his head my eyes found the calendar, and he was right, it was the day, and I, the widow, had forgotten. Exactly a year ago I had sat on the kitchen floor to watch Booth die.

I made a great business of finding just the right vase, and he finished his coffee and departed. I closed the door behind him, leaned my forehead against the cold glass and shut my eyes. How could the date have meant more to someone else than to me? Maybe the struggle was making me so self-absorbed I was obsessed. Survival seemed to have blotted out the day it all began.

I stayed that way a long time, thinking about the life that was left to me, and then I went into the kitchen and washed my face and put the dishes in the dishwasher.

It was beginning to rain outside, but inside the slosh of the dishwasher was somehow comforting. Over the predictable snaps and hesitations of the motor, which I knew like the sound of my own voice, I could hear Booth's amused voice murmuring:

"You had to look it *up?*"

Chapter 10

It was Robert's birthday. He was seventy-six, and I would be his dinner guest for the occasion. I had his present, the book he had wanted, and I was looking forward to a pleasantly low-key evening.

Robert and I are friends and, I suppose, will always be, because in very different ways, we are both lonely. Robert would not admit this if every single one of his fingernails was pulled off one by one, and I admit it to myself only in low moments like driving home in the dark after taking one of the children to the airport or train station to depart my life. Nevertheless, both of us are alone, and because of this I go to his apartment often.

Robert is a legacy. He was a friend of Booth's, and I inherited this friendship. Before, I was simply part of the package; I came with Booth. Now we are both left behind, and this has made a difference to both of us in our separate ways, has left a large hole in both our lives, a hole we tacitly believe will never be filled, though we don't talk about that.

I am always with Robert on his birthday, and this time I was going to be late. Robert, who used to be late himself constantly when he went about, does not like his cocktails delayed. I knew I should hurry, but before I could leave the house there were unavoidable chores.

To begin with, the jewelry had to be hidden. Four houses in the block where I live had been broken into the week before; things that people loved had been removed and never seen again. All of us nearby had been informed, given a police drawing of the thief. Nothing about this had made me feel good.

Gather up the jewelry, all the things from my mother, the silver pin from our twenty-fifth wedding anniversary, the cultured pearls. I stood irresolute, holding the bits and pieces of my life, wondering where to put them. Not in the hamper—that's the first place they look, the police had said so—and not under the sweaters in the drawer. Not in the freezer; not imaginative enough. Perhaps behind the books in the bookcase. Thieves, one supposes, are not very literary and, one hopes, not inclined to browse among books. Right there behind *Martin Chuzzlewit*, in the dust behind the third shelf. It would be too bad to come home and find it gone.

Now the coffee pot behind the curtains in the living room, and nothing remains but the rigging of the doorknob. Attach one end of twine to the hose nozzle on the windowsill when closing the door. A twine disturbed signals a robber at work. Two women had returned early last week in time to surprise the thief and been raped.

No twine, push the panic button. Why do we have to live like this?

Katie lay comatose on the hall rug, gangling legs folded under her, eyes tight shut, pretending she didn't know I was going. After dark she never accompanies me, and she was not going to humiliate herself now by asking. She opened one baleful eye, caught me watching and closed it.

Take care of the house, Katie. You are the burglar alarm, my security system with fur. Bare your teeth. Suspect strangers. Good-bye.

Backing the car out of the driveway, present on the seat beside me, anger welled up inside me. What kind of world is it in which you have to worry that your home will be broken into, lay intruder traps before you spend a few hours away from home? The lighted windows of my neighbors passed in review by the window. Within they sat, reading the evening paper, watching TV, shades tightly drawn, dead-bolt locks in place, smoke alarms at the ready, electric eyes watching each window. Is it possible to circumvent the threat of every danger? If I had money, could I also keep danger at arm's length? But of course trouble attacks where you least worry about it. Perhaps it's better to emulate the young, who know nothing bad can happen to them.

In my purse was the police drawing of the thief-rapist, because Robert would surely take an interest. Stopped by a red light in the crisp dark of the early evening, I thought about that face, so cruel, so expressionless and impassionate. Once I had thought I saw that face in the Safeway, the face of a man buying potatoes, selecting and discarding them methodically, picking the best. I had flattened against the tomatoes, alarm bells going off in my stomach, but another look told me it was not the man. But some delicate equanimity in me had been disturbed, and I slept that night with all the lights blazing. The picture had made it real, and I would have preferred not to see it.

"Does a dog help?" I quavered at the neighborhood watch meeting, but the policeman was talking to someone else, advising leaving a bathroom light on all night. The pretty woman sitting next to me turned and shook her head.

"They say he can get around any dog," she murmured, not unhappy to dispel any hope of special dispensation.

Katie, faithless Katie, would you lick the intruder's feet? Even now she might be peering through the curtains at the picture window at his approaching form, wagging her tail in the mistaken idea that an invited guest, a friend, was approaching.

Stop this. No more nonsense. What will be, will be, and didn't I arrange the twine to forewarn me? Never would I be backed into a corner, left to claim insanity or gonorrhea as the police booklet on sexual assault suggested.

You can't live scared. Life must be worthwhile. Meanwhile there was Robert.

The lobby of Robert's apartment house has always soothed me. Money speaks quietly there, uniformed attendants spring to the locked doors, see me coming on the closed television. The light in the lobby is muted, speaks of vicissitudes smoothed over, hoi polloi excluded. The rugs are deep and luxurious, and never mind the wheelchair ramp on the entrance stairs. Perhaps it doesn't always come with the package.

The elevator ascended silently to the fifth floor, where the ceilings are highest and the view the best. Robert is affluent, unthreatened by any possible reverses, but arthritic and a tiny bit deaf. A fellow club member of Booth's, he had dined at the club table with him, a table known as a club within a club. When the club flag was lowered to half-mast for Booth, no one there had mourned his going more than Robert.

He was coming toward me now, using his walker, an emaciated, elderly gentleman with a taste for gossip and a keen interest in life, though for almost a year he had not been able to leave his apartment.

"You're late," he said, kissing the air beside my cheek and turning to settle ponderously into the sofa. "And what have you brought me in that delicious-looking package?"

Not for a moment did he really wonder what I had brought him. He had been dropping hints for weeks. But it is fun to do things for Robert. He enjoys little presents and stories about what has happened outside the gargoyle-encrusted walls of his apartment house. Robert's friends seemed to have disappeared one by one from the scene, died or moved to warmer places, or simply, finding him hard to deal with and to make hear, dropped him. He sits all day long in his beautiful apartment surrounded by his jade and the portraits looking down from the walls on the Aubusson rug he has willed to some museum, and he is lonely.

He had the book open, and a slow smile was sliding over the wrinkled face.

"Ah, the Windsors," he murmured. "I know I shall be angry about what they say about them, but I shall enjoy it."

Robert's family are visible only in the portraits and the photographs, constantly elsewhere, senders of occasional letters enclosing snapshots of grandchildren. His wife is dead. I cannot imagine Robert married. He seems always to have lived alone in his overheated castle of a condominium, alone but game. Guests at Robert's are always outnumbered by servants.

Cocktail hour was endless. At Robert's there is never any hurry, and the tinkle of ice is the music for the culmination, the high point of the day. Usually drinks are accompanied only by stale peanuts but, on his birthday, Cook had produced beautiful little rounds of toasts with caviar and ground egg yolk. Charlotte, the second maid, was offering them on a silver dish.

Robert refilled his glass with a lavish hand and settled back among the cushions.

"Now tell me," he said eagerly, "what is new."

It is for this that I am asked, and I had been tucking away tidbits all week. I knew which restaurant was good, that the current play at the Winter Garden was held over, that a mutual acquaintance looked well.

He devoured it, listening like an alert elderly crane, head tilted to one side to hear better, all attention. And then he put down his glass and, as we do so frequently, we came around to it again.

"I wonder," he said once more, "why you are working. Didn't Booth leave you any money? It seems so strange."

His curiosity about this is more incredulity than anything else. He does not mean to savor hardship; he assumes that any friend of his must, like him, have whatever money is required. That his old friend should have found himself in a position in which this was not true puzzles him. Money, to Robert, is something one has.

We have been over it before, again and again. He cannot understand it and he cannot forget it. It is not something I want to talk about with him. If Booth did not confide in him, neither will I. It is very hard to make people who have money understand how it is when you don't.

And fortunately there was Charlotte standing in the doorway, announcing dinner, and it was time for the two of us to get Robert to his feet. He is always cheerful about it, rocking to gather momentum, cursing the walker and his legs and the gods responsible for his difficulty, gritting his teeth with the effort of simply becoming once more mobile. But at last he was on his feet, looking remarkably distinguished and proper, and we inched forward into the dining room.

"You don't want to talk about it," he accused as soon as we were seated at the long table agleam with silver and candles.

No, I didn't want to talk about it, but I cannot make him understand why, and tonight of all nights I do not want to be rude. And so I complimented the soup, inquired after his sister in Atlanta, dredged up a joke or two as course after course arrived and departed, each exquisitely arranged on beautiful china bearing his initials. Lilies floated in the Waterford bowl in the center of the table, and Charlotte came and went, and I forgot for a moment what the world outside the door was like.

There was, of course, a very special wine, and Charlotte opened it expertly before his eyes, offered it reverently for his inspection, waiting till he nodded and gestured assent with his fork. She filled his glass, and he watched her carefully, glittering old eyes on the flow of the wine.

"Happy birthday," I said over the rim of my glass, wondering why, at the tag end of a long life, only he and I sat at this table on his birthday. Where were the sons and grandsons and nieces whose faces stared down on us as we lifted our glasses? For that matter, who would be sitting at the table with me raising a glass when I was seventy-six?

He was talking about Barbados, which he had not seen since his legs began to fail him. And then he put down his glass and leaned forward intently, the way he does when he is especially interested, looking the way he does when I know I am not going to like what he is planning to say.

The wine had removed his inhibitions, and he was not even bothering to choose his words carefully.

"Once I asked Booth if he'd ever been unfaithful to you," he said. Who but Robert would say unfaithful? "And he said no. But I don't . . . I can't believe it. Don't you think he ever looked at another woman?"

Out in the hall I could see the portrait of his father done by Rembrandt Peale, and he too seemed to be all ears, eagerly awaiting the answer. I looked at the lilies, and they reminded me of funerals, and the air seemed suddenly close. The enormous candelabra, the tapestry behind Robert on the wall, the magenta draperies on the window beside me all seemed to be hemming me in. But this was his birthday. What does it matter to you what Robert thinks about? Robert is Robert.

I put my elbows on the table and buried my face briefly in my hands, and then I looked up at him.

"He must have known more about that than I," I said finally. "Why do you ask me? Let's talk about something else."

"I didn't know you didn't like to talk about him," murmured Robert, aggrieved, and I wondered why I couldn't give him an uncomplicated answer, tell him the simple truth that no, I didn't believe Booth had had a wandering eye. I will love you till the day I die, he said, putting his arms around me, maybe the last time we quarreled and made it up. I swallowed the last of my wine to wash down the lump in my throat.

But now, behind Robert, the door to the kitchen was opening, and Cook advanced toward us holding on a silver platter a large birthday cake, which I recognized as a product of the caterer downstairs.

She put it before Robert, and he transferred his gaze from me to the flickering candles.

"Blow," I commanded.

He sat staring at the candles as if he had never before seen candles, as if he were a bystander and not the centerpiece of the party, and for a moment I thought something had gone wrong. But then behind him Cook began a steady, rhythmical beat with her heels and the flat of her hand against her thigh, a dark figure in starchy white taking command of the room, sweeping away the words that were hanging over us and the misunderstanding and the absurdities.

"And may Go-od bless you," sang Cook in the clear, true soprano that every Sunday graced the choir of the Fifth Street Methodist-Episcopal Church. "And may Go-od bless you." After a minute Charlotte and I found the pitch and joined in, letting ourselves be led along by the reedlike voice as Robert blew his candles out and laid his old arm on the table, tapping the rhythm with his fingertips.

Deliberately and carefully he cut a piece each for Charlotte and Cook, and they disappeared into the kitchen, the tableau over. In the light of the candles, we sipped our afterdinner coffee from exquisite little cups, discussing politics, the birthday already forgotten. Robert loves politics.

After a while I could see he was tired, and I rang for Charlotte, and again we made our ponderous way up the great hall in reverse, heading for his bedroom. The valet hovered in the doorway, concealing for the birthday his pique at being uprooted from his seat in front of the television.

There was a new painting over Robert's bed, and we stood, we three, admiring it. The room was lined with photographs of people I had never met, pretty girls smiling into the sun in front of sailboats, somebody leaning her cheek on the back of her hand for the photographer, one or two dressed for presentation at court, with long gloves and ostrich plumes. They lined the walls on every available space on the bureau, the desk and the windowsill, each one magnificently framed in silver or leather, all caught at the zenith of their lives, the prime of their looks before time could write anything on their faces, etch disappointments and disillusionments, things that they had learned were not as they had thought.

"Such a gallery," I told Robert. "Should we throw veils over their faces as you undress?"

Robert turned carefully, the walker making prim little half-turns until he could ease himself down onto the bed.

He looked up at me.

"I miss him," he said. "Goddamnit, he was my friend. But if you don't want to talk about him, I won't anymore."

I patted his hand and dropped a kiss on his cheek. I was going. Out of this enormous apartment so full of the past and things that couldn't be said.

"See you shortly," I promised. It hurt to look at him. He looked vulnerable, old.

On the way out the dim lights in the lobby seemed more depressing, and I averted my eye from the wheelchair ramp, smiling good night at the desk man.

When I had nosed the Ford into the driveway, I climbed the back steps and saw at once that the burglar trap was still in place. Mindful of the police instructions, I had my key ready and inserted it in the lock, reflecting that I was lucky to have a key and a door to unlock with it, a life to live, alone or not, choices difficult or not to make on my own. For a while at least I needn't depend on what happened in someone else's life. For which I have to thank, like everyone else, only the turn of the wheel.

Katie rose from the kitchen floor on her hind legs and kissed my hand, and I put my arms around her.

A day or two later a fat letter arrived from Robert, but I didn't even finish reading it. I knew that he would be promising not to speak of Booth again.

And I knew he would.

Chapter 11

THERE WAS something going wrong at the job lately. Nothing I could put my finger on, just something sour about the feel. It crossed my mind that perhaps my future did not lie in advertising, but I was anxious to pretend it did as long as they were. The money was a bulwark between me and a life I didn't care to contemplate. I longed to be the ace writer for Conley Associates. Three days a week, of course.

I wasn't the only one who felt this uneasy chill. We occupants of the cubicles exchanged rumors frequently—over hot chili dishes to keep out the January cold, clustered sotto voce around the coffee machine, shouting to each other over the toilet partitions of the ladies' room. The Head was all there was of management and unlikely to show up in the common ladies', since she had her own.

There were missing faces and new faces. Successive waves came and went.

"Do you like it here?" inquired a bright-eyed new young girl, studying my reflection in the mirror as she washed her hands beside me.

"I like eating," I said carefully. That sounded too bald. "There's a lot of opportunity here," I added, making a great business of applying lipstick.

Worry and the winter solstice had got to me. Maybe we accommodate to living alone, but it needs only two or three days of a houseful of people to remind you of how it used to be when you got down four plates every night and it didn't take a week to collect a full load of laundry. For every hello there is a good-bye that makes it, for a little while, worse than it was before. One gets spoiled with people around. The pain is sharper when they go.

Once more my life settled into a monotone pattern. Get up before it's light, push the dogs into the backyard, eat breakfast, walk the dogs, go to work, rush home to feed them, back to work and home again at dark, exhausted. The future stretched down a narrowing road, gray and cheerless, depressing. Was this all there would ever be?

"I can't be going into another fit of depression," I told Alexia. "I've done that. More than a year now and I'm still afloat. After that you've said it all."

"You've got two nice children," said Alexia in an uncharacteristically mealymouthed manner.

"Yes, indeedy," I agreed, "two nice children. None better, and I'd hate to do without them. And I figured last night having two nice children means one call each a week when we talk five minutes about whatever triviality occurs to us, making contact. Considered separately, that's five-hundred-twenty minutes, or eight hours and forty minutes annually. Plus, let us not forget, two days at Easter and four at Christmas average. Oh, and two at Thanksgiving. This does not add up to a life. Fish swim, children leave home and make their own lives. Forget the kids. It is lovely to know they're there, but one must look elsewhere."

Alexia sighed. Which is as close as she ever comes to admitting unpleasant truths.

"Probably it was New Year's Eve that did it," she said.

Probably it was. Every New Year's Eve for forever and a day, Alexia and George and Booth and I had spent together. Just we four, Alexia and I sweeping the floor in full fig, the men in dinner jackets. Champagne and a cold buffet with candles and flowers just for us. It made us feel clever, secure and superior, unexposed to drunk drivers, safe from funny hats and bores, wrapped in the warmth of close friendship. Every year at midnight we turned on Guy Lombardo and watched the ball in Times Square drop with the coming of a New Year. We made fun of the music, swept the length of the living-room rug in exaggerated Viennese waltzes, laughed at each other and toasted ourselves in champagne. We thought it would always be that way.

Guy Lombardo is also dead.

This year Alexia spent New Year's Eve with her married daughter. She said she had a lovely time, and I didn't ask her what slogan she thought up for the New Year. Sitting rather drunkenly on our sofa and contemplating what was in store for us, we were accustomed to coin slogans for the year ahead. "Seventy-one had better be fun," offered George tentatively, and we had snorted in derision. "Avoid a bore in seventy-four," was Booth's. It was Alexia who thought up "Stay alive in seventy-five." We thought it hilarious.

No slogans for this New Year's Eve. I figured the income tax most of the evening on the dining-room table and then opened a cheap bottle of champagne all by myself, sharing a drop with the dogs. They shook their muzzles, rejecting it. Quite right. Cheap stuff. I went to bed before midnight.

"Alexia?"

"Mm?"

"I think you manage better than I do."

"You keep saying that. Why?"

"I don't know. You just seem to. What was it like New Year's Eve at Alice's?"

A tiny pause.

"It was fun. She had in all the neighbors: she has lovely neighbors. We cooked a turkey, and there was a lot of singing. Some of the men have this quartet . . ."

"Alexia." Sternly.

"Mm?"

"What was it really like?"

"I kept remembering what it was like before we were all lost."

"Work is the answer," wrote my eighty-five-year-old widower friend, the father of a childhood friend who lives in another city. "I wrap it around me like a coat of mail."

The trouble was I could feel the work going soft under my feet, getting worse every day. In the hall now the Head appeared not to see me when we met, whereas before the ghost of an acknowledgment had flickered on her face when I wished her good morning. People were coming and going in rapid succession, and the bookkeeper was said to have told somebody replacements were getting less money. Now it was no longer a rumor of the ladies', it was common knowledge that we were all being evaluated, that deadwood would be pruned, that the Head thought there was much deadwood. Tension crackled in the air at morning conferences. The receptionist quit and moved to Texas, and her best friend reported she had said she wouldn't wait to be fired.

Morale was nonexistent. At lunch hour we job hunted by phone, terrified that the lines would get crossed and the Head would be a third party to the conversation. Telephone calls for departed employees were ordered routed to her office. She walked the corridors frowning, as we pretended not to notice. Property taxes were coming due, the insurance policy on the car was looming and I was nervous.

I redoubled my efforts and, since I was paid according to how much my contributions showed up in final copy, my check was due to be nearly twice the ordinary amount. When the bookkeeper picked up my accounting, she rolled her eyes and clicked her tongue, but I didn't need that to frighten me. I knew beyond doubt that the Head was not going to pay me that kind of money. I thought of reporting a mistake in my figures, but it was too late. My phone was ringing. Paul, the Head's assistant, wanted me to stop by his office.

"She wants to see you," said Paul when I arrived. "I don't know why."

I told him why, and he blinked.

"But she can't reduce your rates," he said stoutly, obviously not believing it.

She could and did. Reduced rates or no job, five

minutes to think it over. The International Ladies' Garment Workers, the leaders of ERA would have wept to see how quickly I went for the pay cut. I was the only downwardly mobile employee of my acquaintance, but it was better than no paycheck. Stumbling blindly back to my cubicle, it was harder than ever to remember a life when money was taken for granted, when I lay in the sun in the tropics in season, journeyed to parents' day at private schools, spent a happy day shopping with friends. What did that woman who used to be me think about?

Everything about the house now reminded me that the future could be a big flat disaster. The sideboard with its big claw feet that had belonged to my grandmother, the little velvet-covered Victorian chair that was my mother's special pet, all the things that had endured safely through the generations now seemed deluded children left with an unfit mother whose roof might be snatched away. I was struck once more with how things outlast people, take from their former possessors a personality that intensifies over the years and cannot be stripped from them though they fall into the hands of charlatans. How dare we buy antiques from dealers? They should require adoption papers.

"Fired?" echoed my acquaintances, "how could that be? You've just started working there." After which they fell to discussing how to make the best quiche. Having with difficulty adjusted to having a friend who worked, they refused to worry about my not working. In any case, work in their lives was something done by husbands, all at the top of their professional careers, to whom the possibility of being fired was as remote as a street brawl on their front porch. One can, they well knew, damage one's health by unnecessary worry.

"Nonsense," they said, smiling. "They're lucky to get you."

I felt as if we were all floating down a river together under our parasols, and I alone knew where the engines were and when the oil ran out.

At Conley Associates there were no such illusions. It was like watching victims drop from the plague. We gathered around the bookkeeper at the coffee machine as if she were a seer with occult powers. What further cuts were planned? In what department? We spoke in hushed voices, never putting a name to a rumor. Who knew who had the ear of the Head, Superwoman ordaining our lives?

I took to staying late to polish my work, and one night, wandering the halls, I ran into Chris, looking if possible more competent than ever. I was surprised to see him, since he had been working some time for another company, though Joan had written that actually Chris might change again. It was remarkable what friends they remained, and I stopped to inquire in friendly fashion what he was doing at Conley Associates. He smiled and said he was moonlighting afterhours on the bank brochure.

I stood staring at him, rooted to the carpet, the carillon boom of his words, delivered in so offhand a tone, reverberating in my ears. The bank brochure was currently my beat.

"I'm buying a house," he said, "and I need more moola." He gave an engaging little throwaway shrug and smiled his really dazzling smile so that he looked like the prototype of the young man on the way up.

This child, this contemporary of my daughter's, was obviously going to come between me and my paycheck. The handwriting was on the wall.

"But there's not enough of that brochure work left now for two," I murmured, trying to keep panic out of my tone.

"It's just for afterhours," he said, putting his pencil behind his ear and realigning the pile of papers he was carrying. "Say hello to Joan for me."

Well, yes, said the other occupants of the cubicles. They had heard that the Head had tried to lure Chris back and that the two of them had compromised on afterhours work. There was a rumor the Head had offered him more money and he was thinking it over. They looked embarrassed.

The Lord giveth and the Lord taketh away. Or maybe Chris did. He got me the job in the first place. Was it not justice that it should be he who took it away? There was no doubt in my mind that I would ultimately follow those who had already departed. Chris would replace me when it was convenient.

I thought about him, bib tucked under chin, stowing away ice cream at Joan's birthday parties. I saw him standing in my kitchen beside Joan, listening intently to me expounding about life. I should have known. He listened too well—I should have seen that—there was something about him even then that made you look twice. He was every teacher's choice for class monitor, every college entrance officer's dream. He was bright, and from the time he turned twelve that smile of his was already flashing success signals. I should have noticed when he stood transfixed by my refrigerator door, spelling out the motto about persistence I had pinned there. "Press on," said the sign. "Persistence and determination alone are omnipotent."

Twenty-three. He was twenty-three, and that was

what hurt. Could it be that he had learned more in twenty-three years than I had in more than twice that time? Was he maybe better because he was younger? Just the negligent way in which he spoke said he knew things I didn't.

I knew I was marked, but nobody came to tell me, so I kept working.

"What do you think, Paul?" I asked him one day.

He shuffled some papers on his desk and looked out the window.

"Just do the best you can," he said and shrugged.

Joan's letter, when it came, said she had cried when she read the news.

"But," she wrote loyally, "if they want him and not you, it isn't his fault, is it?"

Of course not. Except that civilized people who have been friends give some warning, however difficult. Especially if you taught them to ride a bicycle.

Paul quit, and with the new editor, my fate was sealed. I went to him and demanded to know how secure my job was. He led me into the inner sanctum for a conference and the Head looked up, pencil briefly suspended, and confirmed the news that it was time to look elsewhere.

The gymnastics going on in the pit of my stomach surprised me. I had been expecting this moment for weeks, and my stomach was taking on as if it had had no warning. I had a terrible moment when I thought I was going to be sick, and then things steadied down and I was all ice. Reasonably and quietly I demanded severance pay. As a bystander I was quite admiring of how reasonably and quietly. I felt as if I had been in an accident, severely injured but not yet begun to hurt.

"No severance pay," said the Head and went on writing.

Still I did not raise my voice. I remembered to speak clearly and without anger, and when the door closed behind me we had agreed that I would give one more week's work and be paid for two.

On the way home, it began to sink in. Out on the street after a job for which I had considered myself overqualified. Not only that, but replaced by a boy of twenty-three. No visible means of support again, broke, scared, up against the wall. I was beginning to feel the pain, and I was as tired as I ever remember being.

Inside the back door were the sounds of silence and the warm smell of dog.

"I'm fired," I told them. "Through. Out on the street." I pushed them inside and sank into a chair at the kitchen table.

They didn't care. If anything, they were glad. No more long lonely days.

"Dog food will be in short supply," I shouted, anxious to hurt someone, Chris not being handy. Worry, I screamed at them. *No more checks.* Is there a Fired Persons Anonymous where I could get some shoring up? Or a Widows' Rights that would like to know what happened to me?

They yawned, curled around my legs and went to sleep again while I got down the bottle of whiskey. I took two big drinks of whiskey and then I ate a bowl of chocolate chip ice cream. Chocolate chip ice cream with mint, I noticed on the label. After that I went to sleep with my head on my arms at the kitchen table. When I woke up I was very stiff, and all the way upstairs on my way to bed I was thinking that I was walking old.

When the last check came, it did not contain severance and, holding it in my hand, I stalked purposefully down the hall.

"This," I said through my teeth to the Head as she looked up calmly from her work, "was not the bargain."

One of the annoying things about the Head was that she could not be caught off balance. She would review my work, she said, and if it merited it, my severance pay would follow. She had not yet had time to check this week's work.

Payment was not contingent on excellence of work and I told her so. She went on writing.

I knew when I was beaten, but I wasn't telling her.

"You will hear from my lawyer," I said with dignity, turning on my heel.

I didn't have a lawyer, and she and I both knew that if I did, his fees would swallow my check like a frog a gnat. Furiously I cleaned out my desk, dumping everything into a shopping bag including half-eaten candy bars, my coffee mug, paper clips, some useful nearby files. I put my old typewriter into its case and, hoisting it, called good-bye to my fellow workers, now a line of heads appearing around cubicles.

"See you," I called jauntily, and they chorused good-bye, looking embarrassed. And then I closed the door behind me for the last time; unemployed.

Not unemployed, fired, I amended, going down in the elevator. I had never before been fired, and on the only job I had had in thirty years, I had lasted seven months. Seven months, but not eligible for unemployment, I forget why. Out on the streets.

Just as we hit the ground floor I thought about Booth's spindle. I had somehow missed it in the packing, and now strangers—probably my replacement—would impale things on it carelessly, competently, thinking of other things. This could not be tolerated. The spindle must be recovered. It was a possession not for strangers' use. At the risk of an anticlimax, I must return for the spindle. I shifted the typewriter once more and pushed the Up button.

On the way to the elevator the second time, spindle safely in my bag, I very nearly collided with the Head. She had read last week's work, it seemed, and felt it was okay. She was just about to drop my severance pay in the mail.

I reached out a cold hand to accept the check, stashed it away in my purse. Once more I shifted the weight of the typewriter, noticing for the first time what a small woman she was. Small and cold. I looked her over from head to foot and I thought about what she had done to my self-esteem and to my psyche and my bank account and my world. And the teachings of Miss Knox's finishing school for girls and Professor Seagar's dancing cotillion and Smith College and my dead mother and my long-ago nurse all slipped away like a worn garment.

"Screw you, Head," I said and departed with dignity.

Chapter 12

MONEY IS essential, and I was once more without it. I should have panicked, I *was* panicked, but something odd had happened to me down in that cubicle at Conley Associates. Something had risen its head, tentative but growing, that would not be put down. However irrational, I had begun to believe in me.

There was absolutely no logic in this. Being on that payroll had been a fluke that had come about because of Chris. I was still not young in a world in which it is better to be not more than twenty-five if you're looking for a job, love or even second glances. But I somehow had the feeling that, having done it once, I might manage to convince somebody else to pay me for my services.

"But what will you do?" asked Harriet, looking worried, the only one of my friends who understands that money is not a basic and inherent right which comes with the baptismal certificate. Harriet considers that she works. She invests her money, very cleverly.

"Study the want ads," I told her.

Nothing much had changed since the last time I looked. They were still looking for a bright young person willing to grow with the company or somebody with a background in computer programming. But Chris wasn't the only one who had noticed that quote about persistence. I was not going to be a poor little widow ever again. The Head had bloodied me, but the operation had created antibodies.

I began again. I pursued every possible lead, I pushed, I sounded confident when I was scared. I sent out resumés daily, covering up the long employment gap with freelance projects. I learned when the secretaries barring the way went to lunch. When I rule the world, it will be a hanging offense to refuse to disclose whether the boss is in until the caller identifies herself.

But I had no success. I kept trying, getting more and more frightened. And then Joan came home.

There was no warning at all, and I am very good at reading between lines, hearing things people don't say. Just one day the letter saying she'd be coming home alone.

That, of course, is Joan. She is splendid at enduring, pretending everything is going along as usual. There was no hint of why she was leaving Ian. Only that now she had made up her mind, she wanted to come soon, but on standby this seemed to be impossible. Joan grew up in little tweed coats from Best's, saw Europe first from the windows of a Daimler limousine, but now it is always grubby pants with holes in the knees, standby, second class.

I dropped a tear to two on the letter.

Is the end of a love affair any different if you're not married? There was no way for me to tell. When I was her age, we did not live openly without marriage, whatever we did surreptitiously. We had broken love affairs but not broken menages.

"I don't think you take Ian seriously," she had written Booth and me so long ago. "I do. Very." She was telling us then how it was, but neither her father nor I really understood, or perhaps we chose not to.

"You didn't want me to marry him, did you?" she said to me much later. But I never said that.

And now she was coming home. To live with me until she found a job. The house would no longer echo with emptiness. There would be dirty socks, stereo music, interminable telephone conversations. Glasses would proliferate, lights would be left on. But please to remember, only for now. When her paychecks started coming, she would move on.

Never mind about tomorrow. For a while at least I would have someone to talk to once more, someone to share the classified-ad page with. And for her there was now only a winding up—all those books to be wrapped and shipped and that damn guitar. As soon as possible would be best. They say there is no tragedy when we are young, but they lie.

No explanations. Probably he, after all, wanted to stay in France; she chose America after months of indecision. There was no way of knowing. She would tell me when she felt like it. There are some things you do not ask.

The same bed when it is all over? Unthinkable to me,

but thirty years stand between us. And what would her father have thought, that Southern gentleman who died believing that it was man's place to take care of his womenfolk? The father of one of Joan's friends declined to speak to his daughter for a year after she set up unmarried housekeeping with her lover.

I would have to send money to bring her home at once, the difference between the price of standby and first class, in which seats were going begging. She needed a clean break. There was one little difficulty. I didn't have any money, either. The money had dried up.

I sent a cable.

"If you want to come home now, cable collect how much money needed."

The return came prepaid.

"Yes, please," it said and I could hear her distinctive husky voice. "Send $294 to my bank in francs."

Where they had a joint account. Something about her work permit. There was no help for that. The money must be sent. I took it out of the savings account, trying not to think of how little was left, and cabled it to their bank in Paris.

Between mother and daughter there are all those years, and we have been told by the experts that there is no bridging them. Mothers leave indelible scars daughters spend their lives eradicating. Daughters must struggle for identity, shrug off the image of all those dependent years in their mother's shadow. They grow up while we are still trying to buy them Mary Janes, and the idea that they are full-fledged, card-carrying women suggests that our peak years are over.

"Your daughter's house is not your doll house," I once heard a man say to the woman standing next to him as I eavesdropped at a cocktail party. I have no idea what she had done, what went before or after, but the look on her face would have turned butterflies to stone. She knew what he was saying.

Well, Joan didn't have a house and I did, and it was full of ghosts. The dogs and I would be ecstatic to have company again. She and I would be rivals for nothing except maybe a job; we were hardly textbook models of mother and daughter. We had, as a matter of fact, remarkably similar problems, financial and emotional. It went without saying that she would be coming home again. And that she would move on when she could.

I would just have to remember not to get used to her, count on her to push back shadows, make it as it used to be.

She is always the last one off the plane or bus, the last to arrive at a lunch table, and nothing was different at the airport. I had time, watching the steady stream of people who were not her, to wonder if she had missed the plane after all; time to fight down illogical anxiety. Then I saw her, straggling along with the guitar slung over her shoulder, carrying a suitcase and pushing another enormous one, tied together with rope, in front of her feet. She looked small and scruffy and vulnerable. People always take Joan for fourteen, though she is, as a matter of fact, twenty-three. There's something about the way she looks that makes people want to watch out for her. Actually, she has no match for bull-headed determination.

When she saw me she smiled and pointed to the bag.

"They didn't even open it at customs," she said triumphantly.

They were obviously terrified to, I thought, beckoning extravagantly to a redcap.

"What is that rope? A clothesline?"

"A lamp cord. It all fell apart just as I was leaving, and Peter went back upstairs and got the cord from his lamp. He said he didn't use it much anyway."

I gave her a hug, and she felt thin. I forbore asking who Peter was.

"I like your haircut," I said. "Why are you wearing so many clothes? You look like a Chinese coolie."

"They wouldn't go into the bag."

Any idiot would have known that.

In the car, stuffed with her assorted tote bags, erudite paperbacks, floppy hats and a coat I hadn't seen—"secondhand from a flea market, isn't it great?"—I felt constraint. Inasmuch as I have been known to be disconcerted by the steady gaze of a dog demanding dinner, I thought perhaps it was me, but after a while I knew she was feeling it, too.

"The dogs," she murmured, running a casual hand through the new haircut. "How are they?"

"Fine. Kate's gotten big."

We were beginning to sound like strangers stuck in a malfunctioning elevator together. I felt overcordial, a hostess trying to make conversation without mentioning her guest's recent loss of a leg.

"Have you heard from Ted?"

Another damn-fool question. Her brother never writes, not to anyone. We both knew that.

"No," she said politely.

The countryside of Long Island continued to unroll outside the window, bright with winter sunshine.

"The haircut only cost about two dollars because I was a guinea pig in Alexandre's student-training center," she said. "It's layered."

I was hardly listening. I was seeing her all over again in

my mind's eye, pushing the ruptured suitcase tied with lamp cord along the floor of the airport. Did she push it through the streets of Paris that way?

"How did you get to the airport, Joan?"

"Ian took me. It was a friendly parting."

"I'm glad." And glad she had told me. Some of the constraint had gotten washed away.

"It must be lonely without Dad," she said, looking at me for the first time.

I was very busy passing a car.

"Yes," I told her.

I had stretched every nerve for the homecoming dinner. Steak—heaven send she hadn't gone vegetarian like many of her friends—artichokes with hollandaise. Her complexion hinted at a spartan diet, and I longed to fill her with vitamins, meat and fresh vegetables and fruit. Watch it, I said to myself. You have your life and she has hers. At twenty-three you decide on your own diet.

"No brussels sprouts, you notice," I said brightly, but she didn't laugh.

She worked at the artichoke, her favorite food in all the world, peeling off the leaves and sloshing them in the little sauce well of her plate while I babbled on.

It was lovely to see her back in the chair that had been hers since she wore a bib. After a while I told her so.

She looked up, artichoke leaf suspended, and smiled.

"Will you be looking for a job here in New York?"

That was allowed. A basic fact, not really personal.

She put the leaf neatly down on top of the others, a neat pile of discarded leaves.

"Sure. No choice. I don't have any money. But I don't know how long I'll be here."

I tried to peel back the years to a time when I didn't know what city I would be in or what I would be doing in it. It was a long peel, and when I got to her age I couldn't remember how it felt. I like my tomorrows predictable, which they hadn't been lately.

She bent once more to the artichoke while I looked at her with what I thought might be the appraising eye of an employer. My heart constricted at what I saw. She was drooping like a layered peony left out of water. She caught me looking and laid down her fork.

"I think I'll go to bed," she said. "I guess I'm just not hungry. Anyway, by my time, it's midnight."

The steak lay in her plate barely touched, and the artichoke had only been rearranged. She will be better, I told myself. Better and better. I had hoped it would not end in marriage, and now it obviously wouldn't. I was blameless. I had never said a word on the subject. Hoping doesn't count.

"Good night, honey," I said.

When I had cleared up and climbed the stairs to my own bed, I found her crosswise over the covers in her room, still fully dressed, sound asleep in the glare of the overhead light. The ancient suitcase was spread-eagled open in the middle of the floor, and Kate was asleep in it.

I left everything the way it was. Anything else would have been admitting I had noticed.

We were sitting together at breakfast, and I was studying the mail.

"Dear Mr. Mooney," said the message in the window of the envelope, "I believe cancer can be cured. . . ."

I stopped reading and picked up another.

"How can Booth Mooney Get the New 1979 Chisholm

Almanac FREE?" said the stamp on the outside of this one.

How can Booth Mooney still be getting junk mail? Isn't there some kind of amnesty granted to you at the central Junk Mail Office when you die, somebody who says no more, strike his name from the list, he will not be buying in the foreseeable future? Isn't there a moment when the direct-mail specialists call it quits, when pursuit beyond the grave with the hard sell is declared out of bounds?

"Mom . . ."

I stopped ruminating and looked attentive.

"There are some classifieds that call for experience that maybe might do for you. I marked them."

I studied them obediently. Must be willing to relocate . . . modest salary with big future. The house insurance policy was inexorably on the way from the insurance office. If they took the house, we wouldn't be playing games, we'd be poor for real.

"And what about you?" I asked her.

She had a friend who was working on a grant in pesticides and she might know of something. The youth underground takes care of its own. And that left me. Should I try to approach some of my friends' husbands for help? Or, let me see, try to get on in some nice mindless outdoor job like the clean-up detail in parks? I could, of course, be a mail lady. Very good wages, nice uniform and lots of time to think in between pushing letters through mail slots. The possibilities were limitless.

Joan got a job first, at peon wages in a bookstore where all the employees were selling books under oppressed circumstances until they could go on the stage, get their novel written, decide what they really wanted to do, find themselves. On the strength of these wages, she moved into the city to share an ancient Victorian pile with four other young who were delighted to know somebody who could get them book discounts. She had a large, sunny room on the third floor with an elegant nonworking fireplace with exquisite mantel and nothing at all else. I gave her her father's typewriter table, a bridge lamp and a deck chair, and the young people found a mattress in the basement for her to put on the floor for sleeping.

"Found?" I repeated, appalled. "Whom did it belong to before?"

It was of no importance, she said, looking patient; she was lucky to have it. She sat cross-legged on it, her hair falling in her eye, and said she knew she would be happy. From the street beyond the window a neon sign advertising Joe's Pizza winked orange and red, and from the floor below frenetic music drifted up the stairs. I left her a dowry of a bottle of cheap wine and went home feeling depressed.

"What are you complaining about?" asked Alexia quite reasonably. "She's nearby, she can come out to dinner. She'll probably love to come out to dinner. That salary surely won't run to food."

"It was so nice having her here," I mumbled.

"You said yourself she was never home. Shut the door and pretend she's asleep in the bed."

Alexia's daughter was in Chicago, beyond the reach of dinner invitations.

"She's got a job and I haven't."

"Do you want to work in a bookstore?"

Silence.

"You can't compete with your own daughter."

"No." Grudgingly. I wasn't so sure.

"How many times have you pointed out to me it's wrong to live through your children?"

"You know Mary, who cleans for me once a week? She's a widow and she lives with two daughters and three grandchildren. She's very happy. She told me so."

"You'd better come to dinner. You're beginning to sound maudlin."

It was the very next day, in the nick of time, that Louis came into my life.

Chapter 13

It had been a bad night. "Pity us! Oh, Pity us, we wakeful!" wrote Rudyard Kipling, and it might be engraved on my coat of arms. Along with an hourglass with the sands largely in the bottom half and a single ticket stub, probably marked Balcony.

There is nothing like lying awake worrying to color your perspective. The worst kind of insomnia had plagued my night, the kind that clicks you awake at 2 A.M., well beyond the reach of sleeping pills, with all systems go, to lie there alert when the world is at its very worst. There is nothing to do under these circumstances except endure.

On the rack like that, I never allow myself to consider money or troublesome matters. I try to direct my thoughts into other, more positive channels. My mind, wandering around and bumping into fenced-off ground, is very inventive and not very optimistic and had, last night, presented me with the disturbing idea that probably dying my hair since I was twenty-eight when it turned white would cause me to die of cancer prematurely. Lying in bed, tossing and turning, I had considered going white, wondering if it was already too late. How would I like looking in the mirror and seeing my mother? This morning I knew better than to consider it seriously, but the indecision of the small hours had taken its toll.

Toward morning my busybody mind had taken up the question of the strange sound recently developed under the hood of the car. Why had I taken a useless course in elementary electrical repair when what I needed to know was what was going on under the hood? Would this strange clicking evolve into something basic while I was on the road at night, dumping me into the street afoot in a strange area where decent folk were in bed and footpads lurked? Did the odd sound warrant an exploratory operation at Joe's Citgo, where I knew a mechanic? It was a question which had consumed another large portion of the night.

The moon was paling when I turned over and watched it pick out the empty bed under the window. More forbidden ground for the mind, painful enough on a sunlit day, the worst kind of mistake at this hour of the night. The worries perched on the footboard of my bed had chortled, clinging with their ugly toenails and reminding me that had Booth been alive, none of them would have mattered very much. Bad things circle beyond the light of the campfire, but two together scarcely notice. If he had been snoring in the next bed, I would have slept and I knew it, secure in just having someone to share it all with.

Instead, I was facing a new day tired. I was angry with myself for allowing insomnia to get the upper hand yet again, and when the telephone rang and I picked it up, I was pessimistically expecting more trouble.

I was wrong. It was Opportunity, it was the Break, it was Louis, then introducing himself as Mr. Oman. He had heard I was looking for a project, and he was searching for somebody to write the book he planned on sexual mores. Would I be interested? Then we must meet.

My first sight of Louis was a surprise. He was the kind of man I had nearly forgotten about, a rail-thin, elegant gentleman who evoked a world in which things were secure, pleasant and attractive. It was also a world in which gentlemen opened doors, carried walking sticks and wore hats, drank only the finest wine and never never went anywhere second class. Louis lived in a beautiful brick house in Putnam County with his wife Judith, who was nearly always absent on the business of some committee or other having to do with women's rights. Louis was a good deal older than I, and thus made me feel pleasantly young and reckless. And optimistic, because he immediately hired me.

He was also a perfectionist who was never satisfied, but I didn't know that then.

The book was the most important thing in Louis's life, and we worked on it on the terrace of his ancient colonial house with the early spring creeping up the hillside, bringing with it clusters of shadbush and a carpet of green. Sometimes Judith was there, off riding one of the saddle horses in her stock and derby; sometimes she was in Atlanta or San Francisco or Chicago. It didn't matter either way. Louis had long lost interest in her and, as far as I could find out, she in him. What interested Louis was charting the changing patterns of sexual mores from the cavemen down to the *Joy of Sex*. It was all intensely vital to him, and the only thing that interested him about me was how quickly I could absorb this progression and get it on paper.

Deadline was a year ahead, a delivery for which we worked as feverishly as if it were to be tomorrow. Louis was determined to cram into the book every possible taboo, trend and statistic. He was obsessed. He had been head of a very prestigious college psychology department, he had picked the psyches of thousands of students in his long career and the book was the culmination of his life, the distillation of what his research and his students had taught him. When he lectured me, his blue eyes took on a distant look as if he could see the whole panorama of the developing sexual pattern in miniature in his mind. His notes were encyclopedic and mostly impossible to find. He spent nearly half his time pawing through them, searching for the exact reference he needed.

Nothing was outside his scope, nothing escaped his attention, was left unsaid or skipped over. Books with possible bearing on the subject surrounded Louis as sand toys surround a child on a beach, and from time to time we would have to suspend all work while he riffled through them in despair, sure that the exact figures or case history was somewhere in them that would pin down his point. His materials were laid out with no order beyond need. When he needed a file, he played a giant game of Memory.

Weekly I loaded Frieda and Kate into the car to drive

into the countryside, to Nirvana, the house where Louis lived. Since, with Louis, much time was consumed in such rituals as supplying coffee and restorative sherry after the drive, inspecting horse barns and newly painted gardens, I always spent the night. If Judith were there, our conversation was a seesaw between ERA and the changing mores of the young, the politics of key senators on the question of women's rights and the duties of education personnel in teaching the next generation healthy sexuality.

Never did I imagine sex could be so devaluated, so utterly boring, so overpoweringly, depressingly dull.

Little by little, over this mountain of tomes, notes and charts, Louis and I became friends. He was very likeable, generous to a fault if he was personally relentlessly demanding. He welcomed Kate and even Frieda, who was hardly at the stage of life to enlarge her circle of friends, playing her game of blindman's buff tethered under a lilac bush, every rib in the body making a pattern in her fur. Louis's collie, Freud, was an unhappy third to this canine society, trying each time to drive Kate from the place. We observed their relationships, their contretemps and adjustments from our terrace chairs, two detached parents watching their offspring have it out on the jungle gym.

Nirvana was perfect in every detail, a jewel of an old farmhouse renovated and furnished with taste and style and a good deal of money. Louis enjoyed his possessions, but he was casual about them. "Nice things should be used and enjoyed," he would say, closing the dishwasher firmly on his exquisitely fragile wineglasses and relentlessly pushing the button. Housekeeping details appeared to fall on him, yielded by default from Judith. His staff consisted of an apple-cheeked woman from the nearby farm, whom he continually tried to introduce to the mysteries of French cuisine. It didn't work out very well, but it was unimportant. What he really cared about was sexual behaviorism through the ages.

Even Louis could not work all the time, so occasionally he and I and Freud would visit his farrier, his grocer, his wine merchant, make his comfortable rounds before returning for another go at the mores of the Middle Ages. At the wheel of his long black Cadillac, he would draw to a halt in the exact middle of the road to point out objects of local interest. He was obviously the terror of the local farmers, to whom his driving was a legend.

One terrible day early in our acquaintance, we were gone too long and returned to find that Kate, frantic that she might never see me again, had systematically torn the valance from his favorite English wing chair. There she lay when we opened the door, sprawled in the midst of the destruction she had wrought, rolling her eyes up at us, one end of the valance dripping from her mouth and her tail wagging ingratiatingly.

It was beyond discipline—the enormity of what she had done when she was a guest on sufferance paralyzed me. I sank to my knees beside her, gathering up the remnants of chintz all thoroughly mouthed and tattered, while behind me Louis gazed down calmly at the scene.

"It doesn't matter," he said at once, lighting his pipe and puffing furiously. "She was worried, you see, that you had abandoned her."

"Oh my God, Louis," I sobbed. "That beautiful chair. Can you get more matching material so I could have it repaired?"

Forget the state of the bank account. Some obligations rise above prudence.

Louis shook his head.

"She's young," he said. "Look at her. She's quite ashamed of herself. I don't even think she's sexually mature—or rather wouldn't be if she hadn't already been spayed. She was scared. It's understandable. In domestication the dog makes of his owner the leader of the pack, and . . ."

"Louis, she has ruined your chair."

He looked at it awhile. It was irrefutable. It looked like the victim of gang warfare.

"I'll get some pins," he said finally, "and you can pin it back on."

That was Louis.

"But I don't understand," Alexia was saying as we lay sunning ourselves beside her club pool. "He's not interested in his wife anymore. Is he interested in you? I mean, after all, you spend a good many nights there with him alone."

I sighed. I was watching the young girl in the bikini at the other end of the pool and thinking that it wasn't fair that our bodies change so much.

"Alexia," I said, sitting up to apply tanning lotion, "you don't really understand. Opportunity does not equal desire. My God, I'm even beginning to sound like Louis. He is not interested in me, he is interested in sex."

"I see," said Alexia, giving me a queer look.

"He's a nice man."

Actually what Louis was doing was taking all the joy out of the thought of sex for me. Every afternoon when we gathered his books and pencils and my notes and swept the debris off the table and anchored Frieda in the shade of a bush, we stretched sex out like a dead cat on the table and dissected it. We considered how the fact that the early aborigines looked upon menstruation as unclean affected their sexual preference. We weighed the alternatives of recommending that masturbation be thoroughly discussed in family councils as against a strictly enlightened attitude when confronted with a habit. We searched for the statistics on the number of pregnancies occurring when sex was undertaken on impulse rather than as a looked-for event. We weighed and measured sex in all its ramifications so that it seemed to belong only to the biologists as a matter for filing.

I used to bring Louis small presents, like a box of raspberries or a loaf of homemade cranberry bread, but what delighted him most was the story I told him about the seventy-five-year-old widow who had advertised for a sexual partner, no emotional strings. She had had several what she referred to as satisfactory encounters, which she discussed as freely as the weather. Louis was enchanted, begging me for more details. It was no use. I had told him all I knew.

I caught him more than once looking at me speculatively.

"No, Louis," I said firmly. "I refuse to be a case history. Forget it."

"Of course not," he said, waving the idea away with an elegant wrist. "I was only thinking. I have desensitized you, I think. You will admit it, I'm sure."

"Does it show when you look at me?" I said. "I'd like to pass."

"How is it," Louis began one evening, pushing away his strawberries and wine and surveying the purple creeping up the foot of his hill, "that you are so broke?

Didn't your husband have any insurance? You are so wretchedly resourceful and valiant—you bring to mind one of those Brontë heroines come down in the world so they have to be somebody's housekeeper."

It was somehow different than with Robert. Robert would not have been able to understand.

I told him how it had happened: how Booth was sick and couldn't work and had to borrow on his insurance. How he had known he could lick the world with one hand tied behind his back, but he hadn't figured on getting cancer. How he had gone to the office the day before he died. It was the first time I had really told anyone all of it.

Around us the crickets' whirr was a background, and somewhere a dog, not one of ours, was barking.

"I'm sorry," he said at last, and then he cleared his throat and sat up straight.

"Don't ask me about my sex life, Louis," I said warningly. "I'm going to keep my personal privacy."

"I had no such idea," he said with dignity, but I knew he had. "But let's put it this way. Have you thought of remarrying? Someone, of course," with his satyrlike smile, "with plenty of money."

I considered it thoughtfully.

"Not really," I told him. "I'm too busy surviving."

It was odd how the money Louis paid me changed my view of life. It not only made it possible for me to pay the taxes and the insurance, but it no longer pained me to look around the house. Once more it was a pleasure to put away the clean linen, shine the silver, watch the goldfinch competing with the sparrows at the bird feeder. I went back to visiting the Farmers' Market early on Saturday mornings, searching for field flowers to put in my grandmother's bean pot in the sunny window, country sausage for breakfast. For a little while longer at least the familiar things were all going to be safe, and Frieda could continue to stretch her old bones out to warm in the sunny spot on the dining-room rug. I was a going concern again, and it made a fundamental difference.

It was at the Farmers' Market that I ran across Maria again, leaning close to study some pigs' feet, hanging tightly to a child's hand.

We murmured the ritual things that one murmurs when meeting a slight acquaintance after some time, and I told her she looked well. She shrugged and, to cover the awkward moment, I told her about Louis and the book, and she smiled. And there, in the midst of the Saturday-morning shopping crowd, jostled by housewives carrying baskets and young bearded men carrying babies on their backs, we blocked the aisle a moment talking about marriage.

"Do they keep asking you, too?" she asked, shifting a mason jar of canned peaches to the other arm. "They always ask if we want to get married again. They think they would want to if they were in our shoes, so they imagine the same for us."

I was a little lost.

"You mean Louis?" I asked, puzzled.

"Everybody. Your married friends. They all think that remarriage would solve everything for any widow, but I don't know any widow who agrees."

"Wait a minute," I interrupted. "I heard in Florida widows are tipping the doormen at the condos to tell them which have single men in them."

She laughed. Maria is what Louis would call nonjudgmental.

"I dated a man for a while, but it just seemed to bring more complications into my life," she said. "Last week when I wanted to go to a square dance, I called up a man I'd met and said I had tickets. He was very receptive, and it worked fine."

She looked at me for a moment without saying anything at all, and then she shifted the child's hand to her own other one.

"You're basically alone, you know," she said, "and some panic. It's nothing anybody else can work out for you, the way you're going to change and adapt."

I nodded, absorbing it all there by the pigs' knuckles and the goose eggs and the wild strawberry jam.

"My married friends were shocked when I asked the man to the dance. They said if he was so receptive and open, he must be gay. And I said, fine, then he can dance with your husbands."

Louis would have to write a whole new chapter.

Chapter 14

ALL THAT long hot summer I wrote about sex for Louis, but the finished work receded into the distance as the ends of a railroad track recede into perspective. It was like Penelope's web—a labor never finished, which he kept ripping out daily. New sexual mores had to be inserted, experts were consulted who presented heretofore unthought of theses not to be ignored. What had seemed encyclopedically comprehensive the week before became, this week, light, even glib, not worthy of Louis's name. We wrote and rewrote until the words became so familiar they lost their meaning and my one chance of pleasing him seemed by blind luck. Louis was a man possessed, feverishly pursuing Eros down the centuries.

After such a day I would lie in his enormous spare

bedroom, attempting to drain sex from my mind with a mystery. But even there, there was no escape. Parallel reading was left temptingly by my bedside, notes about things forgotten during the day slipped under my door. At breakfast we sometimes considered the sexual taboos of the Mayans over the scrambled eggs.

When the leaves on the maples around his terrace had turned red with the advancing autumn, I told Louis I would have to have a week off.

He was instantly agreeable, instantly solicitous.

"Of course you must have a week off," he agreed at once. "Clear your mind, forget all about the book. You might, of course, want to take along my speech before the Wednesday Club in Atlanta and maybe that booklet from the high-school hygiene class. Other than that, you must put it all out of your mind."

Judith, who was for once making a threesome of our dinner, made small sounds of approval. Louis turned his hawk gaze in her direction.

"Perhaps we ought to take a little trip ourselves," he said, eyeing her as she sat in her beautiful tweeds at the foot of the table. "A sort of early wedding anniversary trip."

The look Judith gave him was first startled and then vaguely unfocused. It made me uneasy.

"When is your wedding anniversary?" I inquired, hoping to divert.

Louis looked at Judith inquiringly, and her eyes took on an inward look.

"September?"

He smiled. Indulgently.

"Try another month," he said, and she wrinkled her forehead.

"October," she said. "October, I'm quite sure. The

thirtieth, I think. Nineteen thirty-four."

"Very good," said Louis. He had lost interest and was helping himself to more soufflé.

"It's hard," said Judith, cutting her meat into meticulous little bites. "Nothing rhymes. But anyway, you'll have to go alone. I have that conference in Dallas, and I'm speaking."

"Of course," said Louis. "Shall we have the coffee in the garden?"

As soon as I could, I fled for a stroll to the remote reaches of the property.

I spent my week with Ruth in the house she had taken on the Cape for the summer. Now that it was fall, she was still lingering on, reluctant to leave and having nothing in particular to do when she got back. Edward was especially busy at the office, so we were alone. For the first three days I simply lay in the weak sun on the beach, pretending to myself that it was warm.

A rest was what I wanted, wasn't it? Absence of the history of sex would be quite enough. We talked about inconsequentials, shopped, played Scrabble in the evening, discussed clothes and recipes—all the things that had consumed my days in my former life. It was like slipping back into another world, contained and undemanding. I knew it was exactly what I needed, and I was terribly glad to have come.

But in Ruth's lovely house the delicate balance of our friendship was off center. Ruth and I are so far apart in our thinking that we come together around the other end of the circle and never have a cross word. But it was her car, her food, her life I was living, and my part had diminished into making myself agreeable. It shouldn't have come hard. The house was a jewel, looking straight out on the Atlantic; the food was prepared by a cook who had had us all gnashing our teeth with envy for years. Anyone should have been delighted with a week of this. I was. Then why was I secretly counting the days till I could get back to my problems, my own little house, even Louis?

Walking a near-empty beach, lying lazily in the window seat reading a book, tea before the fire that felt so cozy in September at the Cape—what more could anyone ask? Why was I out of sync? I thought about it nights as I lay in my bath. The days unfolded, the week was up and I packed my bags with alacrity. I was going home.

All the way back on the plane I puzzled over it.

"I missed you," said Alexia, going way way out on her emotional limb. "I suppose it was wonderful, and I know it was good for you. You had a lovely time?"

"I had a lovely time," I agreed. That's what she wanted to hear.

The house looked modest and familiar when my taxi drew up in front of it, its blinds carefully half-raised to suggest normal life within, the time-controlled lights to thwart burglars glowing. Inside it felt chilly, clammy even, and the refrigerator was empty of anything except a couple of apples and the last pieces of a half-pound of moldy bacon. The junk mail was piled in huge mountains, and the rest was bills. Up in Chatham, Ruth was even now turning on the lights and drawing the curtains against the last remaining light on the ocean, laying the table for a meal in front of the fire, wondering perhaps if the next day's mail would contain a letter from her daughter. The only doubt would be the weather. Would the antique dealer bring round the little gateleg table we had bought together if it rained? A lovely, leisurely, civilized world, threatened by almost nothing. So why was I so delighted to find myself in this cold house alone?

No time to consider that. The birds needed feeding. How had they gotten along without my handouts? The silver had to be located, a giant Easter egg hunt, masterminded by the map in my address book. Little by little I must get it back in places where it was accustomed to dwell, retrieve it from dusty places in the basket of Christmas decorations, the attic, the garage. Toiling up and down the basement stairs, I wondered why, if silver was so valuable, so likely to be stolen from me, I didn't sell it. I had even muttered something of this to Ruth, who I knew would be properly horrified and forbid me to think of such nonsense, but she only lit a cigarette and said, quite sensibly through the smoke, "Why not? You could use the money."

I had been obscurely offended at the time and was still offended. Never. Proper people have silver. Mine had sat on the Empire buffet all my childhood and before that on the buffet of my grandmother. It was part of my life, murmuring comforting things to me. "But you have us still and always will," the silver said. Like me, the candlesticks, the forks and spoons and the children's mugs must take their chances in an uncertain world. Not commodities but friends. Roots.

But it wasn't the familiar things that I had left behind that I missed at Ruth's. It was something far less tangible, something about which I felt slightly apologetic but something that could not be changed. I put my head, which was now beginning to ache, back against the chair, bringing into my field of vision a burned-out light bulb in the kitchen ceiling. I must tend to that, I said to myself, when I had finished my coffee.

After a while I got out the kitchen stool and, standing

on tiptoe, unscrewed the ceiling globe and substituted a new light bulb. Tighten the screws, test the light, presto, a new cheerful glow over the kitchen table. I felt obscurely pleased with myself, oddly triumphant about a thing I had done hundreds of times. I changed the bulbs when Booth was alive. It was no big thing. He was simply not good at anything even bordering on the mechanical.

Ah, but then he would have lingered nervously nearby, warning me to be careful, perhaps complaining that I hadn't washed the globe, admired the finished job. And now, somewhere along the way, I had made a hard forced trade. The habit of counting on him, of leaning on him, had gone. In return I had discovered I could rely on me.

I got up and washed my coffee cup and backed out the car to pick up the dogs. First Kate, with whom reunion is always simply unalloyed frenzy followed by a long period during which she forgives me for abandoning her. With her muzzle glued to my shoulder, we went together to get Frieda, who now stayed at the vet's over vacations. I paid a horrendous bill and carried her out in my arms, shutting her in the backseat where, all the way home, she lifted her muzzle high to howl a high-pitched elderly complaint, telling me of each terrible indignity she had suffered, each deprivation of her freedom. Set down inside the door, she could not rest. Painfully, slowly, hugging the walls, she made a tour of each room, one by one, testing its dimensions with her ear, complaining still.

Kate and I watched silently, and what she was saying was lost on neither of us.

"This is my house," said that high-pitched howl. "I am home again. Here, I am the captain of my soul. Elsewhere, I accommodate."

I gave them both their dinner, and at last they fell asleep, satisfied. I undressed and went to bed early, but before I did I had already thought of several suggestions I could make for Louis's book.

"Did you read my speech?" Louis asked, barely waiting for me to take off my coat.

"Yes," I told him, "but frankly I've forgotten your thesis. I never even got to the hygiene book."

"I thought it fitted in so nicely with what we were saying," he muttered sadly, like a child put off. "Not any of it?"

I shook my head, and he peered down at me curiously. After a while he shifted the papers around a bit and then put down his notebook.

"Tell," he commanded. "There's something on your mind. I'll get the sherry."

I had never thought of Louis as a confidant, this elegant, rich, preoccupied gentleman, but now, with the wisps of his thinning hair falling into his eyes and his thin fingers shifting his precious papers so distractedly, I felt he might be. For the first time his single-minded desire to write the definitive book on sex seemed a reasonable ambition, a contribution to the world, laudable, however precious. He wasn't just looking for a free ride, he who could so easily have coasted.

"I'm not sure I like what I'm becoming," I began.

"No?" he said and he did not smile. "You seem all right to me."

"I loved my husband, you understand."

He nodded.

"But I haven't got him anymore," I said, and as I heard the words it seemed more true than it had ever been, an incontrovertible fact that I had not quite faced. "And I have to make a life without him and I have to work because of no money. And that's changed me."

He nodded.

"Is that bad?" he inquired mildly.

"No. Yes. I didn't used to care that there were a lot of people in this world who just had things handed to them, who just got up in the morning to amuse themselves. I guess I was one of them. I never gave it a thought. And now I'm half-jealous. But more than that I'm half-scornful. And the worst is I've lost the art of making a life with them. I don't enjoy doing nothing anymore. *Me.* Me who used to love taking a recreational stroll in Saks. Me who used to spend happy hours doing needlepoint, lying in the sun on Caribbean beaches. Work is the only thing that makes me feel alive, defines me. And I don't think that's enough."

For a terrible moment I thought I was going to cry.

"You need a sexual affair," said Louis.

"Shit," I said, blinking back tears. "That's all you can think of."

He considered that.

"Well, that's true," he conceded, "but it's what you need right now just the same. Oh, I'm not offering myself. It would ruin our relationship. But you must have candidates?"

"It is not," I said with dignity, "the answer to everything, in spite of what you think. You, of course, are obsessed by it. That's all right, but I still keep remembering love, and it gets in the way. I think my trouble is that I'm growing up in late middle age."

"Possibly," said Louis, turning his glass round and round in his fingers. "Possibly. I do wish I'd met your husband."

I looked off down the gentle hillside and tried to

consider what Booth would have made of Louis.
"He probably would have liked you," I said generously, although I had no idea how it might have been.
I ran my fingers through the fur of the cat who was rubbing against my leg.
"But I'm not so sure he'd like me anymore," I said.

"There is a collect call from, uh, Joan *Moody*," said the operator's voice. "Will you accept the charges?"
Yes, yes, I cried, terrified, and where was the call from.
"It is a local call, modom," said the operator. "The party says she needs her fifteen cents back."
"My God," I said crossly when I finally heard her voice, "don't they pay you anything down at that bookstore?"
"No. They know we'll all move on when we can and there'll be more to take our places. I'll pay you back. I get paid tonight."
I ignored this.
"Have you got rid of the rats yet?"
"There are no rats," she said patiently. "Just mice. I shut one up in my drawer last night by mistake and had to get up and let him out."
"Don't tell me anymore," I begged. "Can you come to dinner tonight?"
"I thought you'd never ask," she said and hung up.

I never understand how empty the house is until one of the children comes home. They make it expand beyond its limits, fill it with noise and silly chatter. I laugh a lot when they are here. People, of course, don't laugh when they're alone, but just having people with you doesn't guarantee laughter. Late in the game now I wonder if I shouldn't have had one more child to expand my life. But that is absurd. Kids owe you nothing. They pass through your life and on to their own just when you get fond of them. One should not be caught depending on them.

The kitchen is filled to bursting when Joan is home. Cooking alongside her is a harrowing experience, but it is interesting. She is careless, even cavalier about ingredients. No capers? Throw in some olives which we happen to have. No zucchini? Well, then, cucumbers are the same color. To a rote cook like me, this is sacrilege, anarchy. I draw back in horror, lecture, gasp. But the cooking itself becomes the primary fun, and later when we eat the food we hardly notice.

I watched her eat, a wing of hair falling across her cheek shiny in the candlelight. She was swallowing it all undiscriminatingly, languid but purposeful, and for a moment I envied her terribly. She knew the future is only a vague rumor that nobody believes, and age about as much of a threat as a famine in China. What if thieves are abroad, money runs out, disease lurks? She was young, and therefore she knew that none of this would happen to her, just as she knew she will never die and cancer will happen to somebody else. What if you have to borrow fifteen cents till payday? Tomorrow will be a bright new day. Whereas I knew that in tomorrow lurks my comeuppance.

It must have been the wine. Usually I hold my tongue.

"Do you ever hear from Ian?" I asked, very throwaway.

"Oh, yes," she said through a mouthful of rice. "Quite often. We're friends."

It was clear that she had put it behind her.

Lovers into friends? I thought about the snapshots I had only that day been rearranging in the ablum—me at twenty-one, wearing my cap and gown the day I graduated from college, ogling the camera, posing, laughing like her at a remote future. The girl in that photograph could never have ended a love affair in friendship. We didn't know how then. Our daughters know better how to handle these things. They don't have to sit home waiting for the phone to ring. Everybody doesn't have to wear a tag Man or Woman.

Something Alexia once said drifted back to me.

"Ruth is such a darling girl," she murmured. "So pretty. Every man in the room sparkles when Ruth walks in."

Ruth is not a darling girl. Ruth is a woman past fifty, slightly inclined to extra pounds. She is a nice woman, still a pretty woman, but not a darling girl. Why do we think we must play these games forever, on into the sunset, hoping to turn male heads, trying to attract male approval any way we can? Shouldn't this sorority syndrome have withered away by now? Why can't we all at last just be people?

"Joan," I said, over my coffee. "I wish there were a man in my life."

She stared at me, mouth wide, chopsticks suspended. Mothers do not speak this way.

"I don't mean to marry," I said. "To take me to dinner. And talk to me."

The night Booth tried to kill himself, he said something—who knows what?—that made me lay down my napkin and come around the table to put my arms around him. It must have been something with the ring of finality. It scared me.

"I can't do it without you," I sobbed into his neck. "Don't talk that way."

But his mind was already set on dying, and I was tearing him apart.

"Don't do that to me," he cried. "You have your whole life before you."

What life? Without him? At fifty-seven?

"Pearl Buck said something interesting in an interview once," said Joan, conveying the chopsticks at last to her mouth. "She said we should never leave things to chance. I guess you can take this to mean almost anything. I don't know why it popped in my mind tonight."

That was the evening I made up my mind I would have to try to put something else in my life besides work.

Chapter 15

"A BIRTHDAY?" Alexia had said once over some long-ago lunch table. "Just another day."

The birthday Alexia was speaking of was probably her own, but it had wider ramifications that reechoed. I rejected what she said then, and I reject it now. I long to introduce her to Eeyore, who announced sadly that his birthday was the happiest day of the year. But he didn't believe it, either.

On the morning of my fifty-ninth birthday, I was determined to believe. Birthdays are watershed moments that induce reflection, and lying in bed for a moment as a special birthday dispensation, I especially wanted to enjoy mine against all odds. A birthday is the most personal of holidays, an annual event in which you stand naked to the winds and vulnerable to intimations of approaching disaster, abandonment on the ice floe, accepting a fading grasp on reality. It is a time, like childbirth or when you're giving a party, that you need your nearest and dearest close by to assure you that it happens to everybody and will all be over tomorrow. I know a young man who is currently being dragged kicking and screaming into his thirties, and unlike his scornful contemporaries, I think of him as a sensible fellow who, earlier than most of us, has figured out what the balloons and the cake mean. How would he like to be fifty-nine, I'd like to know.

I lay there pondering embarking on my sixtieth year. Wonderful things are supposed to happen on your birthday, but unfortunately things often seem to go especially awry. Joan was coming to dinner and bringing a friend—"a homosexual, mother, so please don't imagine some love affair, though he is very nice"—and for the rest, except for lunch with Ruth, I was on my own.

How could anybody think of trying to slide over a birthday unnoticed? You need lights and music and people. It's the kind of occasion that makes you want to confide in strangers, to tell them this is the Red Letter Day so they will say something cheering. I once actually did tell a surprised Safeway clerk I had never seen before that it was my birthday. She froze, hand arrested in its play over the keys of the cash register, face for a moment startled out of its mask of boredom.

"Your birthday?" she repeated slowly, her face gradually coming alive. "Well, now, honey, you have a good, good day all day. Hear?"

Two years and still afloat. Emotions on hold, but perhaps for the best. It doesn't do to examine things too closely unless you're sure what you will find or can stand up to bad news. Building a new life, a new name, with no time left over to consider how it used to be, how it might later turn out to be. Louis, the scratch for money, the broken screen door that needed fixing, the CPA who is in a hurry for the tax figures. Not the stuff of an exciting life, but demanding. And a couple of drawers in the bureau that I still hadn't been able to open because the things there are left over from Booth's life.

Well, so who said you had to do it all at once? One step at a time is okay by me. I lay there listening to the sounds of the house, the funny skip in the alarm clock on the bureau, the companionable hum of the refrigerator in the kitchen, the distant burble of the hot-water heater. Maybe you can make a life without conversation at mealtimes, shared household responsibilities, shirts in the hamper, buses bringing people home, loose change and a second set of keys on the dresser at night. So what if I look out the window and see only the electronically timed lights of my neighbor who is in Florida? Who guaranteed happiness? Survival, maybe, is enough.

I considered briefly what a long way I had come. I wasn't even worried anymore about being found dead in the bathtub. Congratulations, Mrs. Mooney, on your fifty-ninth.

When Booth turned sixty, I asked him if there was any particular pain noticeable in the beginning of the sixth decade.

"I knew what came after fifty-nine," he said.

But we didn't, really. Not him, not me. Thank God.

"Happy birthday," said Joan's voice on the other end of the phone, not waiting till dinnertime, which was very nice of her. Such a warm, nice voice; I felt better already. "I am bringing a cake, so will you please meet us on the bus. I don't mind walking, but the cake is difficult to manage."

It was going to be all right. A cake. People to chase away the shadows, a party really. I shouldn't have worried.

She was rattling on, something about good news.

". . . beginner's salary, really, but I'm pleased."

"You got a raise," I cried incredulously. "I wondered how this call was prepaid. I thought it was because it's my birthday."

I was only fooling myself. My stomach knew what she was saying if my mind didn't. She was about to get her heart's desire and vacate my life.

"I've got a real job at last," she was saying. "On a newspaper. General reporter." Her delight was so palpable that I felt guilty.

"Lovely," I cried falsely. "Close by, I hope." Here, please God, I beg of you.

"Sort of," she said. "Georgia."

Georgia. How much was the plane fare to Georgia? Or the train fare or the bus?

She was rattling on. Only a week before she went. She'd have to buy a car, it was what she had always wanted, she was nervous. Alone again for real, I was thinking; another holiday visitor.

"I'll miss you," I said, struggling upstream in this current of unconfined joy.

"I'll introduce you to Peter. He's pretty upset, too. See you tonight."

Ruth took me to a very expensive restaurant and gave me a perfectly beautiful nightgown, which I would never have dreamed of buying for myself. Staring at it in its nest of tissue paper and ribbon, I told myself that kids were all right when they were around, but friends were what you have to have. They did not go off and leave you at the drop of a hat. They aged beside you, understood difficulties. My thanks to Ruth were embarrassingly profuse.

She waved them away.

"You look so much better than when I saw you before," she said approvingly, and I felt like a good child who has been awarded a gold star for good conduct. "I think the Cape must have done you good."

"Yes. Well, it was nice. And how were the Antilles?" Remembering my manners.

The Antilles were forgotten by now, fading into all the vacations which had come before. And how was Joan?

I hadn't wanted to think about it anymore on my birthday, but there was no escape.

"She's got a job in Georgia," I said, giving it the upbeat lilt so Ruth would know to be glad.

"Great," said Ruth obediently. "But won't you miss her? Doesn't she come to dinner a lot and everything? Is it Atlanta? Maybe you could go to Sea Island or something and she could come over."

Ruth has terrible difficulty remembering that money in this world is not equably distributed.

"No, it's some little place with a population of 2,100. I can't visit her. I'm working on that book."

"Of course"—wrinkling her nose prettily—"well, you have to send her money to come home sometimes."

"Can't hold onto the kids," I said airily, thinking what a lousy birthday this was turning out to be. "It's a great chance for her. She'll be doing everything from sewer-commission meetings to birth announcements."

Ruth looked as if she weren't sure sewer meetings were a real opportunity.

"Isn't it nice," she said, "that she was here for a while anyway. And I suppose being a widow must get a little bit easier after a while."

Ruth's three children live in town and come for Sunday dinner every week. I looked at her and suddenly she seemed so insulated, so wrapped around with love and solicitude, that I felt angry and jealous. It was because of this that I broke a cardinal rule. You don't tell Ruth bad things, things she doesn't want to hear. It distresses her; but I was feeling balky.

"No," I said relentlessly, putting on my coat, "it does not get better. It gets worse. Worse," I repeated crossly.

Ruth was calculating the tip, but she suspended lip-movement adding, looking up startled.

"Worse than at first? But why ever?"

I didn't seem to know when to stop.

"It's not like a broken leg, you know. It's always there, a permanent fact of life. It gets truer and truer."

Ruth was silent, eyes sliding off me uneasily, and I knew I was behaving badly.

"I'm sorry," I said at last, reaching out to pat her arm. "It was a lovely lunch."

All the rest of the day I was ashamed of myself, and so by the time Joan and Peter arrived, I was on my best behavior. I was the model mother of the departing child, I made it very clear that birthdays are Fun and I broke out the best wine even though I knew neither of them would know the difference. Peter was intelligent and diffident, and I liked him at once. He didn't even mind eating steak, which had been a last-minute panic of mine, conditioned by embarrassing choices of menu when entertaining strict vegetarians.

When it was over, I drove them all the way into town, largely, I suppose, to make up for my fit of pique with Ruth, letting them off on the stoop of Joan's shabby Victorian pad and waving good-bye as I snapped the door locks of the car.

"Happy birthday," they called cheerfully, standing together on the steps with the remains of the cake. "It was great. I'll call," bellowed Joan.

I slid through the dark streets with my locked doors, and I knew I would be able to make the adjustment. After all, she was a year in Paris. It was just that I had gotten used to having somebody I loved nearby.

I put my key in the lock, and the phone was ringing.

I don't like phones that ring at eleven P.M., and I took a deep breath before I picked it up. Better to make them think someone was home.

"Is Mr. Mooney there?" inquired a male voice.

The warning flags sprang up like dandelions in my mind. Never admit that the man in the house is not at home, will never again be home, to an unknown voice late at night. An advance check, perhaps, to see if the house is empty, ready for robbery? Certainly no telephone soliciting at this hour.

"May I tell him who is calling?" I asked cautiously, looking around for Kate.

"I'm sorry. I should have told you my name earlier. It's Ken Rossinski in Washington. Booth did some work for us a couple of years ago, and his name came up at the conference this afternoon. Am I calling too late?"

I looked at the azalea plant that somebody had given me for my birthday, and I had time to notice that some of the blossoms were already faded.

"Yes, Mr. Rossinski," I said into the phone. "You are

calling too late. More than two years too late."
And I put the phone back very carefully in the cradle.

It's funny how one accommodates to things. It had been lovely to have Joan just a phone call away, having her come to dinner once in a while, and now I had to get used once more to having her beyond my reach. She quit the book shop, bought a second-hand rattletrap with me co-signing the note and drove off to a new life in Georgia. It's what children do. It just takes some getting used to.

I got out the map and looked at how far away Georgia was, and it was far, a distance not casually to be undertaken by car, not often to be underwritten by a bank account like mine. It was the end of something—or maybe the beginning—either way a milestone. I felt enormously depressed.

That night in bed my father's face drifted back to me. Twenty years he lived as a widower, three of them alone with me. Lying there in bed, I could see him standing among the flowers of my wedding, nearly speechless from the laryngitis he had contracted in prenuptial festivities, kissing me good-bye. "Come home once in a while, will you?" he had whispered hoarsely into my ear, and not until this moment had I understood what my leaving had meant.

I told Louis about it. He was very interested.

"Southern sexual mores, you know, are quite different from the free-and-easy ways of the Northeast," he said. "Communal living is not customary in small Southern towns. The daughter usually remains with her parents until she marries...."

I sighed. He looked startled and then ashamed. He fondled the sleeping cat in his lap and avoided my eye.

"Once," he said in a voice that was scarcely his own, "I thought I'd like a child. It didn't work out that way, and I never think about it anymore."

Louis's children were the statistics we pursued, the far-flung sexual desire that tied together the young of the world in every age. Never having had a daughter, how could he contemplate saying good-bye to one? Whatever his adjustments had been, they were a long way behind him, disappointments and deprivations forgotten in pursuit of abstracts. Maybe in time I could learn how to do this. But however it might be, this gentle, thin man who had everything had been shortchanged.

"Pooh," I said, "she'd be off somewhere now like mine. But maybe Joan will send us back field reports. In the meantime, shall we get on with it?"

"I have this nice place," Joan was saying from the telephone pay station. "The furniture all matches and it's plywood, I think. My rooms look out on a gas station on one side and the thruway on the other. It's really humming all the time and never really dark. So don't worry about me."

"How do you like living alone?"

"Oh, peachy. I can type all night without waking anybody, and I'm learning to make pecan pie. Pecans are pretty high in Georgia, though."

"I'm sending a check so you can come home Christmas. You'll get the day before off, too, won't you?"

She didn't know. She thought so. She would phone again after Monday. What? We had to wait while a passing truck rolled north up the freeway. Georgia seemed a long way off.

"The rent's sorta high," she said in one of the pauses

when we could hear. "I may get a roommate to share the cost, preferably on some other shift. How do you get grease off a stove?"

I told her, but she wasn't really interested.

"How are the dawgs? And you, for that matter?" This last was an afterthought.

"Oh, we rattle around and make a cheerful noise. You left a hole in our lives. But after all, Georgia is closer than Paris, and I'm getting more self-sufficient every day."

I couldn't hear what she said in reply because two or three trucks went by very close together.

When we broke the connection, I tried to imagine the rooms where she lived and where she would sleep and cook the pecan pie and brush her teeth. That was all right, that was allowed, just as I had taken one look at Ted's apartment in Boston. But after that, hands off. Write to them and try to remember Maria, who was left to support three young children alone. You at least, I lectured myself, are free to develop your own psyche, free to make your own career and life.

Was it Janis Joplin or Kris Kristofferson who said freedom's just another word for having nothing left to lose?

Chapter 16

When the world and I were young, romance beckoned at every party, in the club cars of the trains, in the roadhouses where we danced to the nickelodeon cheek to cheek and drank ten-cent beer. At any moment we knew we might catch the eye of a stranger into whose life we would step as casually as picking a dance partner. It was the eternal game we played, looking for magic, the special someone who would, we thought, forever change our lives.

When the war broke out, it was all magnified a thousand times. The uniform of the country was plenty of excuse to strike up an acquaintance. Our world was small and uncomplicated, except by forces beyond our control across the seas, which of course only served to knit us together. Television had not yet homogenized us, and the war was only just beginning to obliterate roots. We always knew somebody from their college, or we knew their sister's cousin and, if we didn't, well, we just got to know them. Maybe the innocence of America didn't quite outlast World War II.

When the war was over the boys came home and we all got married and things changed. The club car on the train was just another way to while away an hour. I guess we weren't looking anymore.

Some thirty years later, alone two years, I wondered occasionally if I shouldn't try to remember how to look.

I wasn't thinking about marriage. I know someone who set out with that in mind and said so quite openly and frequently. She was tired of living alone and went looking for a new husband. She found him in, of all places, the Kupples Klub of her church, which had been persuaded to keep on leftovers of pairs. I can't think this would work out well, spawned in a place where they couldn't even spell, but I wish her joy. I just don't think it would work out for me.

I was, at this moment, quite sure a man was not necessary to define my existence, but something certainly was missing from my life. I had an uneasy ambivalence—fiercely proud of my self-sufficiency and at the same time afraid to be labeled as complete. Marriage was the furthest thing from my mind. What I longed for was a man to take me to dinner.

Alexia was disapproving.

"I never thought of men as more amusing than women," she said crisply. "They talk an awful lot about politics and sports."

I sighed. "They open doors, and browbeat headwaiters who keep you waiting for a table. Sometimes they even

bring you flowers and say they think your dress is pretty."
"I think your dress is pretty. Where did you get it?"
"Pooh," I said.
I never told Alexia, but that's how I happened to go down to the Matchmaker Computer Dating Service.

Right on the face of it, the idea sounded tawdry, and I thought so all the way up the stairs. The Matchmaker's address was tony, but it was a long walk up, which offered plenty of time to change my mind. This couldn't be the way to find male companionship, up these dusty stairs advertising the answer to loneliness. But I kept on climbing, because a long time ago I promised myself that I'd never again be afraid to do anything I had the slightest inclination to do. After some of the verities I had already encountered, everything else looked like duck soup.

I stepped into a big, sunny room and felt better almost immediately. No seamy-looking characters, just a couple of very young, friendly people who smiled a lot. They checked the book and found my appointment—for Harriet Vail, the nom de plume under which I always visit fortune tellers, palmists and matchmakers—took my coat and asked me if I'd rather have coffee or sherry.

"Coffee," I told them. Best to keep one's wits about one in unknown territory, especially if the ground rules aren't clear.

The very pretty girl with the long eyelashes went into the kitchenette to boil the water, leaving me to look over the shoulder of a mustachioed young man who was watching a nervous girl on the videotape explain earnestly to the interviewer that her pet peeve was lack of commitment. He was giving her rapt attention and, watching his total absorption, I felt perhaps the match might be auspicious. But voyeurs were not encouraged, and when coffee arrived, I was beckoned into a back room.

"We're still finishing up with Peter," the pretty girl explained. "Would you like to see the file of some of the available men while you wait?"

Would you like to just slip into this new life for size? The fact that she looked to be almost exactly the age of Joan troubled me, but I told her that if I could look without first enrolling, I would love to see the file. I added that I was still thinking it over.

She smiled reassuringly and said I could look anyway and paused in the doorway, eyeing me speculatively. The appraising look was that of a high-class salesgirl assessing figure faults before sifting the merchandise in the back room.

"What age group would you like to see, Harriet?"

What age group. Take your pick, Harriet Vail, from among the men who have paid money to this girl because they can't handle their own social lives. Men with only first names, men who have checked the rest of their lives below on the street, people whose own worlds have somehow proved unsatisfactory and who need the push of this bright young girl.

Like me.

"Maybe you'd better just bring the file for the top vintage you have," I said as if I were ordering up a meal in an expensive restaurant. That sounded a little autocratic for one in my position, so as a sort of peace offering, I confessed I was fifty-nine.

She smiled yet again to show it didn't matter in the least, life and love were still possible, and disappeared, taking with her all sense of reality. I was Alice down the rabbit hole, expecting any moment she would return to ask me if I could guess the riddle or hand me the little bottle labeled Drink Me, which would make of me a completely different person, sought after and happy.

She was back shortly with a fistful of biographies, to each of which was attached a color photograph. The biographies were preserved in plastic folders, and each contained a thumbnail description—age, occupation, marital status, preference in games and sometimes in women, pet peeves and happiest moments. No last names and no addresses.

I spread the folders out on the table to study them. There they were, perhaps a dozen men staring solidly back at me. Chuck, who had avoided the age blank and listed himself as looking for a lasting, meaningful relationship and had posed for the camera with one arm casually draped on the file cabinet, bravado in his smile. Arthur, fifty-six, an orthopedic surgeon (where in that case were the nurses?) who had two grown kids and thought he was happiest talking to someone understanding. Ron, divorced, no age, but balding, high-school education, pet peeve: people who don't do what they say they'll do, likes his women tall and slender. Howard, sixty-eight, truck driver, obviously barely literate.

Which of these did I want to meet?

We went back into the large, sunny room. The young man with the mustache had gone, but a pretty, pert brunette of somewhere around forty was just taking off her coat. Introductions all around. "Nadine, this is Harriet, who is checking out whether she wants to do it."

Nadine was obviously a habitué of this room. She knew everybody. She was going steady with someone she had met here, but he was not much interested in marriage, and Nadine was looking to broaden her field.

She was divorced; her eyes said she had seen some disappointments in life, but she had a good job as office manager somewhere in Jersey. She got four new plastic sheets with tinted photos to assess, and after a while she selected one of them to look at on the video tape. I got to look, too.

His hair fluttered in a distracting manner. There was a flaw in the tape. He spoke earnestly about his work, the way he felt about people who were not open and trusting, agreed that he liked to dance and said that to his friends he was known as a reliable fellow. He was wearing a T-shirt and a string bollo. His hand went frequently to his mouth.

"I wish he'd smile more," said Nadine wistfully.

The pretty girl in charge said his hair was longer now and that he was more laid back. Laid back? Well, you know, sophisticated. Nadine was uncertain, but she said she would okay a date if he liked her videotape.

Over the rim of my coffee cup, I wanted terribly for things to work out for Nadine. I wanted her to be able to give the steady date who was not interested in marriage the brushoff. On behalf of all the women in the world who are a little lonely and unsure, I wanted her to succeed. I identified with her at that moment in a way I have never identified with Alexia, or Harriet, or Ruth or anybody I have ever known.

I shuffled through my top-vintage pile and produced the biography of Arthur, the orthopedic surgeon. I wanted her to be able to give up her job as office manager and find happiness in the arms of a surgeon. She studied his picture silently, a rather badly developed image of a half-embarrassed, beefy man staring into the camera.

"Too old for me," she said.

The videotape burped, and the face of an uncertain-looking, very young woman came briefly into view and disappeared.

"She shouldn't be shown," murmured the woman on the telephone. "She's met someone, and they've both asked to be taken off view."

I sat quite still, holding my empty coffee cup and pretending to study the biographies in my lap. Ron and Arthur, Dick and Nadine and who knows how many other hopeful people mostly no longer young, and almost, but of course not really, me. All looking for some kind of happiness that life had not dealt us or had snatched away from us. Loneliness was so palpable in that room that I inhaled it through the smoke of the pretty girl's cigarettes, through Nadine's musky perfume. We were as different as it is possible to be, but all of us, in our separate ways, understood about loneliness.

"Ron or Jack been in?" asked Nadine, very offhand.

For the first time the pretty girl looked uneasy, and I was afraid I was going to hear something I didn't want to hear. I held my breath, but it was all right. I had underestimated the pretty girl. Nobody was going to hear from her that she hadn't passed the video test.

"Ron hasn't been in," she said, riffling the files, "and Jack said he would stop by, but he hasn't. You want to meet Norman?"

Nadine looked at her watch and said cautiously that that would be okay. She began to put on her coat, and I wondered how her husband had let this tough-vulnerable woman with the appealing, turned-up nose get away from him. But there are a lot of bummers in life, and obviously he had been one of hers.

I wanted to ask the pretty girl if she had found happiness in the files, but I didn't. Instead I thanked her for the coffee and murmured that she didn't have many men my age in her files. She said they were working on that but it had been difficult, especially since they'd advertised and been flooded with women in their fifties. But they had their sources, and they were sure they could work up a supply. She brought to mind a food supplier remarking that good veal had been difficult to buy recently.

What kind of sources?

Well, you know, churches and places like that. And they were going to advertise some more. I thought of the Kupples Club, and I thought that Pearl Buck was wrong when she said you shouldn't leave things to chance.

I told the pretty girl I'd think about it and asked Nadine if she was going my way. We went down the stairs together, as close as strangers ever can be. We parted on a windy street corner, and she was still looking wistful.

"I hope it all turns out all right," I told her, and I never meant anything more in my life. I really wanted her to be able to give that guy the brushoff.

I could see by the way she said good-bye she wasn't counting on it.

"So okay," said Harriet. "How did it go?"

I wasn't going to tell Harriet about Nadine. It would have been some kind of betrayal. So what could I tell anybody who hadn't been in that large room with the videotape?

"I guess it just comes down to what Groucho Marx said," I told her. "I wouldn't want to belong to a club that would accept me. I wouldn't want to meet anybody who goes to a place like that."

Harriet was silent. We were sitting in her pretty blue living room, sipping sherry and staring at the fire, and a fine rain was washing down the outside of the window.

"Weren't you scared?"

The way she said it, I knew she had been searching for a way to phrase it. I knew it was something that, no matter what happened to her, she would never have done.

I stared her down.

"What? Harriet Vail?"

"I just don't understand how it works," she said. "What man can't just drop by the typing pool if he feels lonely?"

"I don't know," I said and kicked off my shoes to tuck my feet under me while the sherry said comfortable things to me. "They haven't got enough men, anyway. Not enough, shall we say, mature men. They say they have sources they'll tap."

"Who was it said all the good men are married and the rest are dead?"

"You, I guess," I said, watching the fire. "It's a nice line."

We didn't say anything at all for a while, which is the real test of friendship, and I thought about Booth and how it had been when the bus used to disgorge him every night and I would meet him and walk home with him in the fading light with Frieda on a leash, before she went blind and deaf and the whole world went sour.

Harriet is sensitive to unsaid things, and she was giving me an uncompromisingly searching look.

"Is it pretty terrible?" she asked, rearranging the cushions. "You don't talk about it, but sometimes I think about how it must be when you put your key in the lock and walk into the empty house alone with your head high. You're awfully good about it."

I kept looking at the fire. "What's the alternative?"

The living room was very still except for a distant dog barking his head off. I was thinking how you have to go out and do terrible things to realize what a privilege it is just to come home.

Harriet couldn't leave it.

"Maybe I shouldn't ask this," she began, "but are you very lonely? Or does one get used to it? Don't answer that if you don't want to."

Does the hand miss the glove? The sand the push of the waves when the tide is out? Do I wish I could turn back the clock to the way it used to be? Do all the things that used to be make the way it is harder?

"Lonely?"

I turned the word over in my mind as if I'd never heard it before.

"No, I don't think so. Not really lonely. Just alone."

Chapter 17

WHEN I woke up the world didn't look very bright. Outside my window the light was uncompromisingly gray, and as I turned over and stared at it, trying to bring my eyes into focus, I thought it matched my life. "They're wearing a good deal of gray this season, Modom, inside and out. The bluebird of happiness is a silly rumor, really quite outdated. Would you care to try it on for size?"

Blinking sleep-struck eyes, I reached for the reason I felt so particularly bleak. I watched a pair of mourning doves staring motionless in the distance from the telephone wire, and it finally came to me. This was the day I had decided I would have to have Frieda killed.

I shut my eyes briefly against the thought, dreading to put the wheels in motion. My mind unobligingly ran moving pictures of the day we met, Frieda and I, peering at each other over the rim of a packing box in a tacky-looking pet shop. "The mother was purebred," said the fat man, looking dispassionately at the tangle of fur at the bottom of the box. "Father was a traveling salesman." He laughed heartily. "I'm only asking ten dollars."

It was a laugh, the ten dollars. After that was her hysterectomy, her convalescence after the car hit her, the kennel bills while we vacationed, the vet bills, her ophthalmologist. And now the needle that would put an end to our friendship.

I looked over the side of the bed at Kate, asleep on top of my slippers. We were just beginning, she and I. We might in the course of things grow old together. We were both new in a new life, while Frieda was the past, the last link with the time when the house was full of the children and their friends and I got down four plates every night for dinner. "This is the dog who will outlive me," said Booth when we brought her home. Very drunk one night in Mexico City, he had sat straight up in the hotel bed and demanded to know where she was.

I threw back the covers and got up and brushed my teeth, wondering if I were going to be sick. Maybe I wouldn't do it. Her appetite was still enormous. She snapped eagerly at her food after a series of patient peregrinations zeroed her in on it. Going around the upstairs hall, I was reassessing, but from the banisters I could see at once two new spreading stains on the hall rug. She had lost control, an incontinent old lady of nineteen, and there was nothing to do about that. This morning she and I would make the trip, which would be one way for her.

My breakfast eggs stuck in my throat, unable to get

past the lump. I looked out into the gray morning and remembered the times I used to look through that window nervously, awaiting the man with whom I shared the car pool for Joan's school. When he was late, as he sometimes was, I would pace the floor, murmuring piteously that she would be late, that I could not go myself, I wasn't dressed, that I couldn't do it all.

These days I do it all. Make the decisions, a board of directors of one, and then execute them. I gave up trying to eat my toast and put the dishes into the dishwasher while behind me Frieda crouched to produce yet one more yellow pool on the kitchen floor. Beside me, Kate looked up in my face nervously, ears laid back. She was well aware such behavior was frowned upon, yet discipline had not fallen swiftly on the culprit. The world had become unpredictable, and she looked away from my gaze.

One shouldn't get fond of things, much less dogs. Intruders come and take away things you have loved, and the poignant end of the affair is written into the sales slip for every dog who enters your life. The Creator arranged it badly, considering the cruel disparity between the length of a dog's life and ours and the love we pass around knowing this. "It's way beyond stars, toward alleluias," once remarked a head of the humane society whose husband I knew.

The vet would not be in until ten o'clock. He was unavailable. I could have an appointment at 10:30. By 10:30 I might change my mind again, but she was not going to spend her last hours in a death cell awaiting the needle. We would wait until the vet was there.

She had fallen asleep in her accustomed place in the hall, back to the closet in the corner. Sensing expectation in the air, Katie was staring at me hopefully, begging to be included in whatever expedition I was planning. I looked at the clock and put my arms around her. She would go, too, so that on the way home we would have the comfort of each other.

When it was finally time to go, I picked up Frieda in my arms, no heavier than a dried lamb skin, and carried her to the car. I drove very slowly so that she would not fall off the backseat, and now all I wanted to do was get it over with.

"I'll go with you when the time comes," Harriet had once said, staring at Frieda lying so thin and ancient in front of the fire. But I had never really believed the time would come, and, if it did, I knew that the last mile is the one you do alone. No bright chitter-chatter. This was a family affair.

We came to the mailbox you can use from your car, and I pulled over to drop a letter to each child into the slot. They were my apologia, my dissertation on old age, my notification that they had lost an old friend.

I left both dogs in the car while I made the arrangements. A nice middle-aged woman turned from the typewriter to check my name, retrieved Frieda's file from the closet and looked up brightly.

"And what can we do for her this time?"

There was only one answer to that, and I told her she had come to be killed. Like Frieda's ophthalmologist, I am not much for euphemisms. Nice plain labels go down better. I try not to fool myself.

The receptionist nodded and indicated a chair. I hoped it wasn't too cold in the car and tried to think about something else. The something else turned out to be that at least animals never have to anticipate pain and death.

The vet, a gentle, patient man who truly loves his patients, came out of his office and beckoned me. I opened the car and let her come out on her own, keeping control with the leash. She made her last puddle, and I thought that when it was over, I would bury her blue collar with the simulated jewels under the hickory tree where the last guinea pig before everybody grew up is buried. There would be nobody to attend these ceremonies the way there had been for Pig. "Come in, come in," I had cried, tears streaming down my face, to the young girl who had rung the doorbell in the midst of it all. "We're just burying Pig."

The girl had been a friend of Ted's and a very suitable mourner. I never saw her again, but I think of her sometimes.

The vet lifted Frieda up on the examining table and ran his large hands over her ribs and lower abdomen as she stood there, patient and dignified.

"What seems to be the difficulty?"

I managed to get out that she had lost control of her bladder, and I feared it was the end of the line.

He began to unbuckle her collar.

"Nineteen, I think it is," he said to nobody in particular. He handed the collar with the leash to me and put Frieda under his arm.

"She's pretty old," he said, "but why don't you call me in a couple of hours."

All the way home I drove with one arm around Katie, trying not to think about anything at all. Not very much later the receptionist called.

"Frieda has cystitis," she said. "She can come home day after tomorrow."

"But you'll just have to nerve yourself up to do it all over again," protested one of my neighbors across the street when he heard, looking at me so that I was in no doubt what he would have said if he had stood in that vet's office.

And maybe he would have been right. I don't know. Maybe I would have let her go if Booth had been alive. Alone, I held her in this world by the tail, shoring up each infirmity, struggling to underwrite more years for us together. I do not say it is right; it's how I am. "You fought for him," said the doctor, extending his hand in farewell to me in the hospital corridor after the postmortem. "It will probably help later to know that."

I didn't like him from the moment I saw him standing there on my doorstep, but then it was not required. Mutual regard was not in the contract. It was his little jeweler's glass, his expertise I needed. He represented, actually, a triumph, for his kind were booked everywhere three weeks in advance. The price of silver had soared into the stratosphere, thievery raised to a high art. Clever men with sophisticated means of dealing with locks and electronic eyes were abroad, and every household treasure, the insurance companies had nervously decreed, must wear a current price tag.

He seated himself, with his assistant, at the claw-foot dining-room table and began to peer through his glass at the accumulated pieces of my life.

"One child's teaspoon with cloissoné picture and legend, Sweep the cobwebs from the sky," he dictated to his assistant. He lowered the glass and caught her eye over the gleaming heap and barely concealed a smile.

The smile irritated me, but I said nothing. It was only necessary to get on with it. The household that held me together was under a stage of siege. Eight houses within sight had been stripped of all their treasures. For days now I had considered how it would feel to come home and find everything gone. Each must be enrolled on a little list of household effects, opposite a figure that this man would set.

"One silver-backed mirror and brush, initials EB, poor condition," he droned, and his secretary scribbled.

It is true that I used that hand mirror of my mother's to hammer a nail into my bedroom wall so I could hang a picture. It was a picture of some boy whose name I have long ago forgotten, but I remember the excitement when I used the mirror to drive the nail home. I am totally responsible for the pockmarked back of that mirror. It is none the less dear to me. Four-H youngsters must feel this same loyal coiling of the nerves when the judges mutter their cool assessments over their brushed and shining heifers. What do judges know, or for that matter, jewelers?

The appraiser looked at his watch and reached for another piece. It was the celery dish marked Pinehurst Spring Tournament, March 8, 1912. The name isn't filled in because my father, having reached the semifinals, forgot and went home, leaving his opponent standing on the tee. They sent this after him.

"Gorham, number A9879."

And the silver card case that dangled from my mother's wrist back in 1911, the year she was married.

"We're running into the second hour. I just wanted you to know."

The candelabra Booth gave me for our twentieth wedding anniversary.

"Rather damaged, I'm afraid. Dropped?"

"Let them take mine," growled Alexia fiercely. "They're only possessions, only chattels. I can hear you saying only a few years ago that you wanted no more silver to push through life with your nose."

"I don't want any more," I said. "I would just like to keep what I have."

"The important thing is supposed to be human relationships," said Alexia, "not things. You know—love and trust and somebody who answers the phone and will come and get you if you have a flat."

I didn't answer that. Both of us were thinking that was not for us. Not anymore.

"It was you who told me not to cry over anything that can't cry over you."

It was all true. I said those things. Good, solid, becoming sentiments. I can't think now why I said them.

"You're divesting yourself of things," I said accusingly, "and making me feel like Silas Marner. And when you've gotten rid of all the things, what will you have left? It's awfully hard to curl up to long distance love and trust. What will matter to you?"

Below the belt. George had not been dead very long, not long enough for Alexia to figure out the answers to any questions, what she really thinks about anything.

"You didn't give the silver much thought before," she said.

"I took it for granted. It was always there. That was nice. That was home."

"Do you care about it more now that that man has told you it's worth so much more than you thought?"

Touché. When the unlikeable man and his secretary had left the house, he had handed me the paper making it clear that the silver was worth more than we had paid for the house. Next door it was the same, the same in the houses in the next block. It was possible for me to gather it all together and take it downtown and sell the lot and stop worrying about money. What did I actually care about my grandmother's teapot when my only memory of her was of a formidable woman lying upstairs in the great sleigh bed, pointing out to my father that I had a runny nose?

I cared. I have some friends whose silver was early stolen, and they took the insurance money and went abroad for several months. In the fullness of time the police found the lot of it and offered them the chance to buy it back, but they had spent the money, and besides, by then they had found they got along quite nicely with stainless steel. Everybody said how brave and kept loaning them surplus silver, the way you dig in your closet and give poor people whose houses have burned extra clothes. They gave a lot of parties and showed slides of their trip.

I'm just not made this way. Anchorless, I look to the things around me to support me. I like having the chair my father's roommate at college gave him when he married, Booth's silver-backed military brushes in which still lingers the faint scent of his hair. I'm no gypsy, ready at any moment to move on with a rolled-up poncho. These unnecessary old things are the points of my compass. I have an emotional investment in them, and I would be bereft without them.

"Such sophisticated burglars," moaned my neighbor over the hedge. "They say they bring the fence with them and he tells them which is worth taking and what not to bother with."

What's worth taking in my house would melt away like a thin ice coating. Like fine wine, it would not travel elsewhere. Take this spoon engraved Marjorie, 1885. It belonged to my aunt, my father's maiden sister, a terrible old lady whom I nevertheless liked. She couldn't bring herself to leave her father's house even when she had spent all the money he left her, so she just kept selling off the furniture. She was born in that house and she expected to die there. She lay in her huge brass bed in the living room and the entire upstairs was as unknown to her as the steppes of Siberia. She sold off a lot of things that didn't belong to her but to the heirs, but she ordered the silver brought and put under her bed so she could watch it. This spoon was there when she died.

You had to know my aunt to care.

Alexia, in her new phase of traveling light, is unconvinced.

"But how often do you use those spoons and things?" she persists. "Do you ever take that one of your dear Auntie out of the drawer even to look at? And what about your father's napkin ring?"

Well, not very often, it is true. Maybe once in a while, when I give a party and I serve curry and have little dishes on the side. Maybe then I get out a lot of spoons I mostly don't. And maybe not, too.

But I know they're there.

Chapter 18

I AM planning to form a Society for the Restoration of Actual Holidays, an Alternative to Three-Day Weekends. It will be known to us members as SRAH, which I admit is a mouthful, and I am aware that it may encounter some resistance. The travel people and the department stores will send us hate mail, but we will rise above it. If George Washington, standing noble in the bow of his rowboat en route across the Delaware River, could have foreseen that his birthday would be marked as a moveable feast to suit merchants' sales charts, he would have lowered his eagle gaze in shame. He might even have lost his equilibrium.

The birthday of our first President actually fell on Friday this year, which would have made an honest three-day holiday about which I could not have complained. But the government, in its mysterious and obdurate ways, had again interfered with history, moving the anniversary to Monday. Thus, though I had already got through two days of the semi-isolation weekends now impose, a third loomed. Louis was off visiting friends, my own were cloistered with their families, and one simply cannot work all the time. Stretched before me was a desert of a Monday, unbroken by lunch with friends, mail possibly bringing checks, conversation with anyone but dogs, not even the cashier at the bank or the man who was putting new lifts on my shoes. In another life I had directed not only my own days but had a word or two about those of three other people.

Actually I had the twenty-four-hour flu, but I didn't know it when I woke. A good day, says the pillow on Harriet's sofa, is one in which nothing hurts. People who live alone have no way of knowing they have a common virus, that the entire third floor of the Bigelow building downtown had the same thing last week and recovered. They start wondering if they have something terminal, if this is the moment to take stock. I lay there feeling the day was already starting off badly.

It was all a little harder to bear because Joan was, after all, not coming, had not come. Contemplating this looming third day of the holiday, I had written a check and sent it with a scribbled message to take a plane, a train, a bus, a donkey, hitchhike, but come home. She had agreed, but late Friday night the phone had split the peace of my bedroom and shattered my sleep so rudely that, in my haste to find out what the catastrophe was, my groping hand had found only the ornamental marble owl by the bedside lamp, into which I had repeatedly bawled a nervous hello. By the time I discovered my mistake and got the telephone receiver instead, I had not been able to absorb much beyond the fact that she had missed the train and would come next weekend instead.

Next weekend was several years off.

I reached for the bedside lamp, the better to see my watch, and when I settled back on the pillows, felt faintly dizzy. Sudden movement, I decided, but when I got up to shut the window, I knew things were not going well. I brushed my teeth, but I didn't bother with breakfast.

I thought about my funeral.

"But we didn't even know she was sick," they would all cry, dabbing their eyes. "How brave she was! Not a word to anyone. I suppose," looking nervously at Ted, "it must have been days before she was found."

"Days," he would agree. "She was quite desiccated." Dry-eyed but shattered inside, he would avert his gaze.

The dogs were not having any of this, or anyway Katie was not. She crouched, awaiting the familiar progression of the routine that means the leashes are going to be gotten down, the boots put on, the whole delicious routine that is as dependable as sunrise, sunset, to put in motion. How do you explain to a dog that you have the flu, no walk today? I capitulated before that steady stare, put on my boots and got down the leash.

Slow progress up one block and across the street and turn toward home. Twenty minutes paced to Frieda's measured steps. I was no longer watching scenarios of my death; I was concentrating on not falling down. I felt lightheaded and gastronomically uneasy. When the door closed on us, I went straight to the sofa because it was nearer than the bed.

By noon I was able to manage a cup of tea and a Saltine. The dogs ate heartily and went to sleep. The smell of the dog food unhinged me, but after a nap I felt better, enough better to wonder where the neighbors all were and what they were doing. The entire world seemed to be on hold.

I longed for the sound of a human voice, though I was not up to staggering out to vie with the hordes in the pursuit of Fantastic Holiday Bargains. Dial a Prayer, maybe? Or my astrology forecast? If I wasn't going to die, I needed to talk to somebody. I was suddenly starved for human contact.

I got up and assembled some of the income-tax figures, and when I next surfaced it had started to snow. It was drifting down lazily but steadily in that peculiar gray bright light that I remembered from my childhood upstate, when the snow arrived in October and stayed through March. Booth and I were married on the ninth of March, and as we walked out of my father's house hand in hand, the snowbanks were higher than my head.

I sat staring at the hemlocks putting on their white dusting, and I knew I had to get out of the house. I took a sip or two of skim milk and put on my boots and the hood I keep for moments like this when it is very cold. I had a little difficulty starting the turgid engine, but at last it responded, and with Katie beside me in the seat, looking eagerly ahead at the drifting flakes like some ship's figurehead, we set off together for a look around Bloomingdale's.

Spring in Putnam County arrives just as everyone has given up hope, and its early harbingers were creeping up Louis's hillside. The last of the snow was melting away, the air had turned soft, and Louis's book was at last perforce coming to parturition. The source of my income was drying up once again, and it was time to look ahead.

"Dear E. Mooney:" began the letter from the bank.

Your application for a Master Charge account has not been approved. You have not had two open accounts for a full year, one of which is time payment. Although we cannot comply with your present credit needs, we hope you will avail yourself of our many other banking services.

What is this, dear First National? Don't you remember me? I'm a widow now and I need your help. I'm the one who has been keeping those credit cards busy at nine department stores for over thirty years and, at least within the last twenty, never been late to pay. Well, yes, those charge accounts were in my husband's name. I didn't know it mattered. You're not going to take them away from me, are you?

Once I was a respectable matron. Now I was an upstart with no credit references. The paychecks were about to thin, money would be harder to come by and the credit door was slamming.

What about the house, First National? I remember very clearly that my name was on that mortgage. I own it all now, free and clear. You mean it doesn't count because that's joint credit and that file is closed? Yes, yes, I know that it is illegal to discriminate because of marital status. What about all of us who stood before the minister thirty-five years ago and merged our identities, including our credit? Before this antidiscrimination act?

The car, then. I paid cash. It's mine. It says so right on the registration. Time payments? I can't afford 18 percent annually. You discriminate against cash customers? And women who use their husband's names?

Why can't I have a Master Charge like everybody else?

You can't cash a check without one when you're out of town. The man who changed my flat tire yesterday expected me to have one. Tish, Joan's classmate, has one and she's twenty-four. My son has one. Harriet's maid has one.

"A lady," I can hear my English godmother saying, "has her Christian name in the paper only when she is born, marries and dies." Dear Aunt Millie, if I knew earlier what I knew now, I'd be a Lucy Stoner.

Only the doctors wrote our Christian names on their charts when I and my contemporaries were getting married. After all, men do remarry, and it is well to know whose body you are working on. At the bank possibly they knew our names, but not always. Finance was largely then the province of gentlemen. We were Mrs. Jos. Roberts or Mrs. J. L. Lewis, and that's all they needed to know. Ordering our slipcovers or our household linen, we signed our Christian names because we knew it wasn't proper to sign our husband's—which of course we appended in parentheses immediately afterward so they knew who would pay. For the rest, our first names were for friends.

Dear Joan, I wrote, be very careful when you fall in love. Oh, I don't mean that, I mean about your name. Let him give you his heart and his money and a wedding ring and Valentines and candy, but never his name. I pray Saks and Lord & Taylor will never discover your father is dead. I shall be stripped of everything but my library card.

No credit, no job and once more an uncertain future. I hadn't been looking for work for a year, and I had gotten used to having money in the bank. The party, however, was almost over; the book was all but done.

Right up to the deadline Louis was amending, altering, adding to, revising; but there was an end to even this. We wrapped it up one sunny afternoon and posted it to New York. For better or worse it was over, and he looked bereft. In the proofreading, perhaps, things that had been forgotten could be appended, he murmured wistfully.

I felt unaccountably melancholy. Somebody else was going out of my life. Already I could see him focusing on the farflung bookstores that might sell this book. He had a friend on the faculty of Berkeley, a cousin in New Orleans who was well connected, friends in Idaho who had interests in a bookstore. He would make the rounds, take copies, his usual peregrinations would take on meaning. I felt sorry for Freud, who could look forward only to lonely evenings and dog-sitters.

Louis was going to make a marvelous talk-show guest. He would be urbane and witty but informed about the subject the talk-show hosts know is box-office boffo. He would take from sex the smirk, the dig in the ribs, and would bestow upon it the dignity of scholarly history, the sweep of human urges affecting civilization. And he would love doing it. The book would do well.

He didn't ask what would happen to me. Louis had tunnel vision. He handed me the final check, and there was no drama in our good-bye, from which trailed numerous tendrils of details as yet not ironed out. We would lunch occasionally, perhaps have dinner together, with or without Judith, but the thing that linked us was over. His eyes were on distant horizons, and I needed new work.

"So much for that," I whispered in Katie's ear as we rolled down Nirvana's imposing driveway for the last time. But she was interested in the wild rabbits and did not seem to care, either.

It was the end of something, and there had better be a new beginning. And soon.

This year, this year for sure, I had to paint the house no matter how frightening the price. This summer I had to figure out how to bring in some more money. There was a small leak around the stack in the rear roof, oozing stains into my bathroom ceiling. What I needed was another Louis.

And while I was at it, some way to put joy into my life. I wondered how the woman who had joined the Kupples Klub was making out with her new husband. I wondered if he was paying repair bills and if she disliked any of his habits, in which he was no doubt set due to age. Should I stop pursuing the dollar and join the church, or Parents Without Partners (was a child led by the hand an entrance requirement?) or study yoga with an eye to finding some companionship? "Would you marry again?" I asked a pretty widow I met at somebody's dinner table somewhere. She thought about it awhile. "Not unless he were very *very* rich," she said finally, giving me a dazzling smile.

I lowered the want-ad section and caught sight of the twisted crab-apple tree in the side yard. It was just about to burst into bloom, just a spit behind the first crocus, which was struggling up through the crabgrass in front. The sparrows had returned to nest again in the vent of the exhaust fan above the stove, secure in the knowledge that they had a patsy landlady who would not turn on the power till the brood was raised.

I really needed another Louis.

Freelance writer, more or less regular basis, ecological magazine, moderate pay. Phone for appointment.

The moderate pay was the clinker, but it was better than nothing. I could keep looking, but in the meantime I would give this one a try.

Shabby office, rickety elevator, lobby directory heavy with do-good organizations. *Quite* moderate pay, probably. My heart sank, but you never know. Maybe I could do the work without devoting much time and add something else, too.

The receptionist was definitely not glad to see me. Somebody had obviously told her to type this before she went home, and it looked to be a close call. She looked up briefly. Mr. Renquist? Down that corridor, over there. She didn't even bother to ask if I was expected.

I was worried about my hair. It had been very blowy on the street, and only the models in the shampoo ads look well with their hair streaming out as if they had just emerged from a wind tunnel. I halted and searched in my bag for the comb. Don't tell me if it doesn't count how you look. I struggled with the snags, work samples clutched between my knees. I wanted this job.

A tall man built rather like Ichabod Crane came loping around the corner, avoiding me neatly and passed on.

"Mr. Renquist?" I called after him, and he turned and peered back at me, running a long hand through rumpled hair.

"Yes?" he said, and it was clear I was an impediment

to an appointment elsewhere, an obligation he had forgotten about.

"I had an appointment," I said. "You know, about the free-lance work."

"Damn," he said, furrowing his brow and frowning. "Of course, I remember. The only thing is I can't see you now. Financing calling. I go when they call. Why don't you leave your resumé on my desk?"

Chapter 19

We were sitting in the elderly bar of the Stanwix Hotel above my office, holding hands, and the jukebox was belting out "Don't Sit Under the Apple Tree with Anyone Else but Me." The Japanese had just capitulated, and everybody around us was very drunk or well on the way. Across the room a fat man gestured to the bartender and raised his glass to Booth.

"I want to buy the soldier and his girl a drink," he roared. The sleazy woman beside him nodded.

The bartender brought the beer, and from across the room Booth raised his glass to the fat man, looking embarrassed.

"I feel like a damn impostor," he muttered through his teeth. "I spent the whole war in the public-relations office. The rest of the time I was explaining what p.r. is."

195

Outside in the street the world was going mad. Strangers were dancing and hugging each other and throwing confetti and kissing passing girls. Around the bar a group was trying to get through a chorus of "Bluebirds Over the White Cliffs of Dover," in direct competition with the nickelodeon. We kept holding hands because it was the ending and also the beginning and a solemn, drunken moment. The ending of the war and the beginning of us.

"Will you marry me?" he said through the cigarette smoke, as if we'd never discussed it before. "And never let anybody or anything else come between us ever? That is, the moment my divorce is final."

"Of course. That's understood," I said.

We all knew our Noel Coward letter perfect then.

Well, nothing came between us except those damn cigarettes. I stopped staring out the window and resumed opening the letter from my college-reunion chairman. Oh, God, could it already be forty years ago? And now somebody called Skippy wondered if I would be able to make Hamp for reunion and what committee would I like to serve on? It would be a great opportunity to catch up, exchange personal data, swap pictures of grandchildren and no doubt mention modestly about work on the committee for the Improvement of the Arts and for Better Schools for the Socially Deprived. Tish and Martha and Scooter would all be there, and even Ann was coming from San Francisco.

Well, no, Skip, I'm afraid I won't be going back to Hamp this spring. Only the successful, the leisured and the solvent attend college reunions, curious from the warm nest of a stable life about what happened to everybody else, stealing sidelong glances at name tags and secretly wondering if this stout woman with gray hair could be the same with whom they drank a million Cokes before Sociology 11 on Greene Street. Spring won't find me in Hamp, Skip. I'm scratching for a job now that I'm pressing sixty. Of course, if you have seminars by graduates, I could give you a nice talk on Making It Without Love or Money After Fifty. It has a nice ring. You could set it to music.

Unbecoming and bitter. One of the least lovely qualities is envy, that sophisticated form of self-torment.

It's the why-me syndrome. Occasionally it rears its ugly head. Especially when my past life crops up.

The phone was ringing, and I knew it was the Daughters of the Purple Heart calling to ask if I had any cast-off clothes. Not this time, Purple Heart. I seem to keep wearing my clothes.

The phone was insistent.

"Hello," I barked into it.

"Elizabeth?" said the curiously deliberate voice, "I like what you left. There's not a lot of money, of course. There never is in ecology, but if you want to try to work with us, you can." He cleared his throat and seemed to have lost interest.

"Oh," he said and it was clearly an afterthought. "Evan Renquist. At *Wilderness Ways*. You were down here."

I said I was glad he liked my work, and I felt sure we could work something out. Always take all you can get when they're passing out opportunity.

My first thought when I saw Evan in his office was that he would never turn out to be another Louis. This man's clothes hung on him as if he had borrowed them and they regretted it. One button was coming loose, and his gray hair was rumpled. He had the look of a brooding vulture, and when his eye met mine, his expression was intelligently melancholy, as if he knew things he would rather not.

"I'm sorry about the last time," he said, apparently to the wall. "It was out of my control."

I said brightly that I quite understood. I hate myself when I am maneuvering for work. I am alert and capable and very self-assured and it is really very tiring, this trying to appear more self-assured and clever than you really are to impress someone who could make a difference in your bank account.

He seemed lost in his own thoughts, and I, with difficulty, waited out the silence. I have a regrettable tendency to fill in conversational voids, a tendency which has to be kept under close rein. I think I learned this deplorable habit sitting on the little gold chairs in Professor Seager's cotillion, tongue-tied with terror lest one of the reluctant horde of small boys being urged toward us should not choose me. I observed in those days that the most successful girls chattered up a storm as they plumped their skirts and eyed prospective partners. It left its mark.

He seemed finally to recollect that he was not alone. You can do the work at home, he said. It would be reasonably steady, if I continued to suit, if I caught on to the style and audience of *Wilderness Ways*. He rummaged in a drawer and came up with several back issues for samples. He slid them across the desk and mentioned a figure that was only slightly better than my worst fears. Was that satisfactory?

He looked at me closely, and for a moment I considered telling him that both he and I knew that the money was the pits, but that I was in no position to argue.

"It's satisfactory," I said, and he nodded, looking oddly relieved. I put on my coat and departed.

Evan and I were for a long time strangers. For weeks I knew nothing at all personal about him, though I saw him often. He had a cold, it had been rainy upstate, the odd hint of Boston in the *r* was actually New Hampshire, he was deaf in his left ear from a war injury, speak up. I never imagined a life for him out of that office, a home, a wife, children, a dog. He was simply the man I had to please in order to eat regularly, and I looked upon him as a sort of unpredictable village elder who might at any moment throw my words back at me and remark in that deliberate voice that I had been missing the mark lately, perhaps I would be happier with another magazine.

I kept picking up the work and delivering it, feeling grateful that it seemed to suit. For the rest I was preoccupied, wrestling with another roadblock I had never anticipated, one that was making me feel that one more piece of familiar ground was crumbling away. The husbands of my friends were reaching retirement age and turning their faces back to where they came from, or to the sun belt with its kindlier taxes. Just as I was getting started, they were finishing—and threatening to leave me bereft.

One after another they murmured of the lure of trouble-free condominiums, crime-free residence in the sun, where the only tie to where we all lived now would be the pension check in the mail. Their bones, they said, smiling to show they didn't think so for a minute, were getting old. The children were gone, the old house was too big. They were thinking of pulling up stakes—not yet, perhaps, but one of these days.

I scoffed. It would pall, I said vehemently. To get up in

the morning and wonder only if the sun would shine, to pursue the perfect seven-iron shot through life on the fairway winding its way past the picture window of their ranch house; these things would not turn out to be enough. They listened and smiled, protected by being part of a pair and by savings, threatened only by what the doctor might find at the annual physical. Not right away, of course. . . .

It was the blow I had not foreseen, and it undermined me. Retired couples are as complete as honeymoon couples, dependent on no outside friends. They go together to the A&P, on little errands to inspect new ways to save energy on the porch windows, to the galleries to see the new exhibit. Once more I saw that I was stag at the dance, out of order, even more extra than before. Nights when I woke for that wretched hour or so that afflicts us poor sleepers, I thought about the Kupples Klub and the acquaintance who had found happiness in its roster. When I went to a cocktail party and met a mutual acquaintance, I inquired eagerly about this woman's new married life. I was ashamed how pleased I was to hear that it had not all been so entirely easy. There was trouble about whose furniture should be sold, whose children they should visit. Remarriage, when you come fully equipped, is not as comfortable as the first time around, in spite of what Frank Sinatra sang.

Sundays Ted called from Boston, voice vibrant with the excitement of a career on the rise, a nice balance between love and work, with simply being young. *Wilderness Ways* sounded like opportunity to him; I had plucked the coal from the fire one more time. I searched my mind for something amusing and flip to say, something to assure him that Aged Mamaji was paddling her own canoe just fine, but a terrible sense of the futility of the struggle weighed me down. I burst into tears.

Across the miles of telephone wire or whatever miracle connects callers from different cities, he was puzzled and anxious.

I made him, shamelessly, into my free psychiatrist.

"I expected to do without your father," I sobbed in the phone, "and without money. But I can't do without friends."

But I had friends. He recounted them all like a litany, consoling, patient. Moving away? For the young there are always new friends waiting in the wings. The young have a terrible time summoning up even the sketchiest idea of what it is like to know that when a friend of thirty years walks out of your life, there will not necessarily be a replacement.

Everyone I knew was already looking ahead. Harriet was renting a Florida condominium for a couple of months and invited me to visit. I could bring my work. I stole a week and the plane fare from my savings and flew to West Palm Beach.

We drove up the Atlantic shore under the blue blue sky, past the fast-food joints and the small shops. Every day the sun shone, and we carried our tanning lotion to the pool, unplugged our minds and sprawled in the beach chairs a thousand miles away from *Wilderness Ways* and my typewriter. The white egrets made a flowering bush of the mangrove beside the front door, and the twisted ficus trees marched down the beautiful avenue like slaves in chains lining up for review. We watched the gulls overhead with their black feet tucked neatly up against their breasts and once more I was a girl of eighteen, sitting beside my father on the terrace of a hotel in Fort Lauderdale, sipping Coke and stirring it idly with a fresh pineapple muddler.

He was staring at the waves lazily spilling themselves on the beach.

"Let's go home," he said, "where the real people are."

I didn't understand him then, but now at last I did.

It was Cape Cod all over again. It was not the tag end of my life. It was only the beginning, and I wanted to go home and get on with it.

When I next brought work to Evan's office, he was on the telephone and gestured to me to wait. There was no particular place to sit down, but I took some back issues off the one chair he wasn't occupying and sat down uneasily. Was this the time he would tell me that he had found he no longer needed free-lance help? I studied the back of his head, which he had swiveled around to me to view as if, invisible to him, I would no longer be an eavesdropper on his conversation.

He was talking to the printer, and to divert my mind I tried to make of him a small boy growing up in New Hampshire, tall and gangling even then, gray eyes still hopeful and eager. But he seemed always to have been a middle-aged editor, a born coper with an irrational and unpredictable world. It was no use.

He put the phone back on the cradle, swiveled around and looked at me.

"You're tan," he said, and it was almost an accusation.

"Yes," I said. "I've had a week of life among the leisured classes."

He smiled, a brief wintry smile, but I liked it better than the one-dimensional ones I had been seeing so frequently of late. He looked down at something on his desk, and my stomach went cold as I saw it was my last piece.

"Was there anything wrong?" I quavered, forgetting the masquerade of assurance.

He looked up at me abstracted, momentarily puzzled, and then shook his head.

"Oh, that," he said. "No. Your piece was fine. I was just wondering how to ask you to have lunch with me."

Chapter 20

THE FIRST thing I thought was that he hadn't said Let's lunch and talk about the work. Inside my mind, red warning flags were being shaken out everywhere. Keep the business and professional lives neatly separate, because if anything goes wrong socially, chances are it's bye-bye paycheck.

The second thing I thought was that it was terribly nice to be asked. It is noticeable how male friends with whom you lunched before you were a widow disappear from your life when you are single. And here was this strange, brooding vulture of a man standing there looking expectant, wanting to take me to lunch. He hadn't leaned on our casual business relationship, he had said flat out with no dependent clauses that he wanted my company. It was a handful of diamonds.

"That sounds nice," I said politely.

We walked along the avenue, past the club where Booth had lunched every weekday of the last years of his life and where the flag had hung at half-mast when he died. I looked away, and we turned into a small bistro beyond and slid into opposite sides of a booth.

"Drink?" he said, raising his eyebrows.

"Drink," I agreed. This was not a man exactly afflicted with logorrhea.

He told the waiter to bring two Dubonnets and, with the gray eyes otherwise engaged, I got a chance to look more carefully. In his office he had seemed part of the desk. It was his home, his roost. Here he seemed someone I had never met, a stranger from the Matchmaker Computer Dating Service groping for common ground.

"The money," he said after a thoughtful sip of his Dubonnet, "is lousy." It was going to be about the job, after all, and I felt disappointed. "But perhaps you don't really mind. Maybe it doesn't matter. Maybe you're rich and do this all for kicks."

It made me laugh and surprised a small, wintry carbon copy of a smile on his own face, a smile laced with puzzlement.

"I'm a widow supporting two dogs and a house I can't afford," I told him. "It matters."

He was sorry to hear this. He hadn't any control over what he could offer. He looked deep into his Dubonnet as if the answer to this deplorable situation were somewhere hidden at the bottom of the glass.

"It must be difficult," he said. "How long?"

"Two years and four months." I still knew to the day.

"What do you do when you're not trying to earn money?" he asked, proferring the menu.

Exactly. What do you do? Besides eat and sleep and work. Tell the man.

"I think about where to get more work," I said. "It's what I do in life. The sum total. Actually you have put your finger on a flaw. I am bothered about it."

He studied me silently and quite openly, as if I were an anthropological specimen with which he was not familiar.

"What about you?" I asked. If he could probe, so could I.

"Me?" He seemed surprised to be asked. He shoved his water glass a bit to the left and then back again. "Why, I'm trying to write the great American novel, of course. Isn't everyone? Weekends and, if I'm not too tired, after dinner. Sometimes I get myself out of bed early before I have to go to work."

Who cooked the dinner and handed him his plate, piled high and warmed? It was inconceivable that he had a cozy house somewhere in the suburbs. If ever I saw a loner, it was he. He looked as if he had a graduate degree in aloneness.

The waiter took away the menu and brought us steak sandwiches. He ate absently, as he did nearly everything else.

"And when the novel is a large success, will you quit *Wilderness Ways* and lounge in your country pied-à-terre wearing cashmere sweaters and drinking Cutty Sark?"

"Yes," he said. "Naturally."

"Will it be soon?"

"No. Things get in the way and keep changing the way I think. I'm not in the mold. Have you ever noticed it takes guts to be no longer young?"

I have, oh, I have. Every night when I wake.

"It gets more complicated," I said carefully. "Things get less black and white, and the reasons don't seem so clear anymore."

He smiled his wintry smile, and it had a nice, companionable warmth. We lingered over the coffee in the dark cool, while outside the window the sun made little shimmers rise from the cement of the sidewalk. The people walking by looked like survivors of combat duty, enduring until the next door to air conditioning should open for them.

"We'll lunch again when you come into the city," he said, counting out the tip. It was not an invitation, it was a simple statement of fact.

As I often do when I climb into bed, I put on a little dab from my precious bottle of Rochas perfume. Very very expensive. Buying it was an indiscretion that occasionally overtakes me when I know better, because I love lying in bed wrapped in all the perfumes of Arabia.

"Show me something new, something fresh and exciting," I said to the young woman in the perfume store. It was Paris and the world was very simple and safe and I was going to bring home some presents and something for myself. The children stood on tiptoe, anxious to smell, too, while the woman brought out seven little bottles and touched the stopper of each to my wrist, the hollow of my elbow, the backs of my hands.

I couldn't make up my mind. I told her in my schoolgirl French that I would go away and decide and come back, and she nodded approvingly. *"C'est different, ce parfum, pour vous, madame, que pour une autre femme."* She stoppered each bottle and smiled dazzlingly. *"À bientôt,"* she said, waving to the children.

We walked the sunny street for a few moments and

settled ourselves, a very American family of four wearing tweeds and shiny shoes, at a little outdoor café with umbrellas and potted plants and ordered some silly orange drink called Pfft or maybe Psst, all around. And still I couldn't decide. This wrist, that elbow, which would make me more desirable, more femme fatale? It was an important decision to make in Paris.

When we finished our drink, I got up and went around behind Booth's chair and put my arms around him and said, with my wrist under his nose, cheek to his, "Which one?" He took the cigarette out of his mouth and sniffed his way up my arm like a hungry lion sampling a Christian.

"This one," he said with decision. "I want you to smell like this. Always. Sexy. Rich."

As the Frenchman at the next table looked on approvingly, he planted a kiss on the wrist with the right perfume, and Ted and Joan burst into laughter and had to smell, too, and we hurried back to the parfumerie to buy a large bottle and some for friends, skipping part of the way because we were young and in Paris where we never expected to be.

Damn it, I said, as I turned off the light and threw the evening paper I had been reading on the floor. Useless to look back, nothing is served. There is no going back, not ever. Understand?

I turned on my side, and it was then that I noticed from the ceiling reflection that the pattern of the lights in my neighbor's house had changed. There were no longer two little squares of light below and one above, but one below and none above. My neighbor was in Spain. The house had been left in my charge. I was watering the poinsettia that she had nurtured since Christmas, taking in the morning paper. I stared at the little square of light, and something moved across one on the ceiling.

I got up and parted the curtains of the window overlooking her house. The light patterns were certainly different. And to whom did that little blue sedan belong, the dusty model resting at the front walk? Her car was safely in the garage. I had watched her put it there.

I shrank back against the wall, staring at Katie, asleep beside my bed on my slippers. Wouldn't she know if something was wrong, intruders were next door?

Down the block they had broken in and taken everything only the week before. This week two houses behind me had been robbed. A young man with a gun and blond hair, who had pistol whipped the occupant, said the police. Was he there behind the square of light that I could no longer see because of a trick of the blind? On the floor, Katie slept the sweet, quiet, undisturbed sleep of a well-fed dog who has had a run. Perhaps a bulb had burned out in the second window. I was imagining things. Women who live alone get absurdly nervous. If something was wrong, Katie would let me know.

The light from the streetlight picked out the empty bed by the window, and I shut my eyes. He would have been no help, no help at all. First it would have been impossible to wake him, make him understand what was wrong, and then what could he have done, a sleep-befuddled man in a pair of rumpled striped pajamas, that I could not do alone? Automatically I looked in the corner for the empty soda bottle he had kept with which to confront an intruder. An absurd kind of slingshot against a gun, then and now.

I mustn't let myself get out of hand. Worry feeds on worry, and reason departs. I burrowed down under the covers and thought hard about what kind of vacation I would take if I ever got hold of some money.

I must have dozed off briefly, because it took me a second or two to identify the steady, low-key rattle. I sat up in bed and looked at Katie, now on her feet and growling, listening to something beyond the reach of my ears. The hair was standing up on the back of her neck, and somewhere within reach of those pointed ears, something of which she disapproved was going on. Over the purr of the air conditioner, through a closed window, something was happening that had brought her to her feet to emit this low, well-bred rattle in the back of her throat.

I stared at her transfixed, and she returned my gaze with flat, yellow eyes that were turned inward. Very carefully I got out of bed and, keeping well away from the window, peered cautiously at the next house. Nothing had changed. Or had I perhaps, after all, caught a glimpse of something moving in the background?

I crept over the bed to the nightstand and dialed my neighbor's number. Across the seventy-five yards or so that separated us, I could imagine the phone ringing unanswered. I replaced the telephone in its cradle and sat, cold with anxiety, in the middle of the bed, considering the embarrassment attendant on false alarms, the ridiculousness of women who worry unnecessarily. After a while I leaned over and dialed 911, the police emergency number.

I could be wrong, I began, apologetic now that the die was cast, feeling the way you do when you get an emergency appointment at the dentist and the tooth stops aching and the pain is only a memory. Perhaps it was Emily's son, who must certainly have a key. Then why doesn't he answer the phone? Perhaps Katie was growling at a raccoon intent on the trashcan, perhaps I was simply jumpy, nervously alarmed.

They had heard it all before. I had pressed the buttons which put it all in action; there was no getting out of it. "Name, please," they said briskly, and I could see the pencil poised over the blank white report sheet. Address? Telephone?

I told them everything they wanted to know, and when I hung up I sat in the exact middle of the bed, hugging my knees and waiting. I could hear nothing, no sirens, no noises of approaching law. I knew that they had seen through the nervous imagination of a lone female and shelved the cry for help.

I got up and went to the window and saw that I was mistaken. The show was already going on below, a production I had set in motion without understanding how enormous it would be, how embarrassingly lavish. Cars drew silently one by one to the curb in the shadows, flashlights signaled each other from the shrubbery, two men were converging on the back door, hands on holsters. The hair on Katie's back was as stiff as a porcupine's, and I sat by the window in the dark and prayed that they would find someone and I would be vindicated.

They moved out of my sight, and after a minute or two the doorbell rang. I padded down the stairs in my bare feet, holding fast to Katie's collar. Did I have a key to the house? Across the street, I said, pointing and oddly breathless. They stood in a polite circle in the dimness of my economically 40-watt porch light, competent, taciturn and helpful—on a fool's errand initiated by me.

They came back when they found nothing, to report that Emily's son had come in to change the lighting timers and borrow her car in exchange for his. The blue sedan was his, ma'am, but listen, thanks for being on the alert. Yes, ma'am, crime was a terrible thing these days. Can't be too careful.

When they went down to the police car, they were talking among themselves. I knew what they were saying. Old bat got jumpy. Get a certain amount of these. I felt a terrible shame, and the scent of Rochas had faded on the pillow.

"But you were told to call first and not hesitate. You told me that yourself," said Alexia comfortingly. Alexia had dead-bolt locks and bars on convenient windows, strong locks everywhere.

"There were three cars," I said, "and men with drawn guns. It looked like 'Dragnet.'"

"Good," she said, leaning back among the pillows of the couch. "It shows you get good service. I worry about you with your damned twine around the doorknob and the windows all draped in shrubbery."

"My windows are burglar-proof," I said with dignity. "They have been painted shut for years, all but two. I do not care to take on the image of a jumpy old busybody."

Alexia would never have done such a thing, and we both knew it. She does not inconvenience doctors or policemen or veterinarians except when she is writhing in pain, and then only if it is between nine and five P.M. I, on the other hand, feel that taking Hippocrates' oath and wearing a police uniform make you subject to calls in the night.

"Has it ever occurred to you that there might have been someone over there?" she said kindly. "Someone who slipped away as they were arriving? And that you did it?"

At the hairdressers' when I next arrived, they were abuzz with the newest robbery. The victim had been planning a party—lamb chops, asparagus and strawberries—and at the last moment discovered she was out of cocktail crackers and had gotten into her car to run to the Safeway to get them. On her return she had surprised a burglar, who was just packing up the remains of her astronomically valuable flat silver, including her mother's service, and all her jewelry. Told with a gun to sit down and shut up while he finished, she surreptitiously slipped out of her engagement ring and kicked it under the sofa. But he saw. Made her get on her hands and knees to retrieve it.

Delicate shudders passed like a wave among the clientele. Did the newest victim have security systems? What time of day was it? What was the address? How did he get in?

Backcombing my hair, my hairdresser whispered in my ear that she was ordering barred windows and an electric eye that day. Her husband traveled. She was afraid to be alone.

Recollecting my own solitary status, she paused, comb suspended over my upended hair, watching my reflection in the mirror. "But aren't you afraid, living there all by yourself with no security? Just you all alone?"

"Never," I said. "Not too much spray, please."

Chapter 21

IN THE little group around the grave, only Cook and I were weeping. Possibly we were the only ones lacking in control, possibly we felt at that moment we had lost the most from our familiar world. Bearing up is good form; the stiff upper lip shows class. I don't know why I am always in the back row weeping shamelessly.

Robert was dead. He was gone for good from his lair in the ancient, gargoyled condominium, taking with him my memories of a world where the only things that mattered were being ornamental or not boring. All the things that mattered to Robert are no longer much approved of, have gotten a little musty.

"Dust to dust," intoned the young minister wrapped in his black robes, "ashes to ashes," spilling a little cigarette ash on the top-model casket from Newbury's undertaking showroom.

"Was the death expected?" inquired my neighbor as I gave him a lift early in the day on my way to the funeral.

Yes. No. Well, not by me. I never know when to let go, never expect death. Everybody else had long ago accepted that Robert was dying. For months he had spent the better part of the afternoon in bed, napping, writing long screeds on thick, off-white stationery in his spidery hand to friends in other cities. But the tinkle of ice when day was done had always found him perched among the pillows of the sofa in the library, William Buckley's image flickering on the TV screen, vodka bottle within reach. I rather thought it always would.

The dinner invitation at six o'clock brought my first cold foreboding. Robert never dined early. Part of the mystique of his world was fashionably late hours; a six o'clock summons was for children. Yet here I was being ushered in with the sun still high and not to the library at all but to his bedroom. There he lay in his monstrous brass bed, propped up on pillows and wearing his very best brocade dressing gown. Freshly shaven and smelling of expensive shaving lotion, but abed nevertheless.

"Dahling," he had murmured as I leaned to lay my cheek against his.

But what is this, I wanted to know. Not up for dinner? Not ready for the cocktail hour?

"It's a bore," he said, dismissing it all with a wave of the hand. "You don't mind having a tray in here with me, do you?"

No, I didn't mind. Robert and I were bound together by some sort of thread that still puzzles me. There were others he loved more, as there certainly are in my life, but each of us depended in some odd way on the other. When Booth was alive, we dined often with Robert, at large, chic dinner parties with place cards and extra waiters, exquisite freesia and anemone arrangements in the delft vases, Château Latour in the tall wineglasses. Alone, I was demoted to small evenings and after a while to dinner *à deux*. To Robert not matching was perfectly okay, but at parties younger women, preferably very pretty, were better.

"But what is it?" I had cried in alarm, feeling one of the dependables in my life threatened. Robert was a premier dependable, a hoarse voice on the telephone, issuer of invitations that I did not exactly long for but without which I would have felt a lack. And here was Robert not demanding vodka, which was already late in arriving, not asking what was new and what I had been doing, leaning back in the pillows and looking tired.

He hitched the pillows behind him, and I could see it was an effort.

"Nothing," he said. "Symptoms are so tiresome, don't you think? Did you stop to buy some raspberries from the vendor on the corner as you came in? It must be raspberry time," he added wistfully, his eyes on the curtains that met the top of the air conditioner, blocking the smells and the sultry torpor of the street below.

I sat in the little gold ballroom chair beside him, and after a while Charlotte arrived with the rolling bar and parked it by the bed. I poured and handed him his Bloody Mary, but the hand that accepted it was languid and looked suddenly thinner. I noticed for the first time that it was deeply etched with veins, the hand of an old man. In this breathless room where the air-conditioning unit could not deal with the heat from the streets below, he kept a thin blanket over his knees. I laid the veins of my own wrist against the side of my icy glass and smiled at him brightly.

I chattered, as I am expected to do on these evenings, but he was not really listening. The pulse in his forehead throbbed visibly, and for the hundredth time I wondered how old he was. We will never know, any of us who are left. It was whispered at his club that his passport, obtained before birth certificates were common, had been fudged for years. Robert avoided talk of age, incriminating reunions and dates that pinned things down, and in the presence of his wicked grin, we were all distracted from facts. "I'm not seventy-five yet," he would say, and a week later, forgetting, "I don't know what I shall do about my seventieth." If the truth was written on his tombstone, I would never know. I wanted him to keep his secret into the grave.

"Drink your drink," I said to him that night, a mother admonishing a child. He had frightened me.

He looked at the drink in his hand a moment and put it down beside him on the silver tray.

"I hurt," he said. "When I cough, there's blood. It makes terrible stains. I think there is something badly wrong with me."

No, Robert, no. I need you. I count on you.

"Does the doctor know this?" I said, calm and detachment wrapped around my words like a gift package presented in a hospital. "When did he last come?"

The ghost of that grin dismissed doctors as a class.

"He says whatever occurs to him. Doctors write you off when you're dying. They like to make miraculous cures, have grateful patients fawning on them."

Dying? The fear and the drink inside me tumbled around like wrestlers.

"We'll get a second opinion," I said fiercely, forgetting my masquerade. "It's done all the time. They do wonderful things with laser beams or drugs or God knows what. I know a very good internist."

Charlotte's huge form loomed in the doorway, carrying a tray that she put in Robert's lap. A tiny table appeared in front of me, laden with pink beef, little round new potatoes, wine, chocolate mousse.

"Robert, you must not give up," I cried. "We'll find a specialist in whatever it is." It was Booth whom Robert had loved, but we were the leftovers and we had grown accustomed to each other. Who would send me letters explaining what he meant to say, tell me about life in Newport before reality intruded, sit beside me under the chandelier and discuss whether Zelda Fitzgerald had any talent? "Will you promise me to ask for a second opinion tomorrow?"

He picked up his fork and put it down again.

"Maybe I have TB," he said. "Didn't your mother die of TB?"

Yes, yes, of course she had. Lived for years with it before that, though, and now TB is easy to cure.

Don't go, Robert.

We picked at our food, talking of things that didn't matter, and the air conditioner faltered like an iron lung and resumed its well-bred hum. Surreptitiously I wiped a delicate dew of sweat from my forehead. The demitasse Charlotte put beside me set off little wisps of steam, and I looked away.

"I have a present for you, if you want it," he said, shifting his lanky body to the side of the bed painfully and swinging his legs over the side, testing before getting to his feet. I handed him his walker, and he hoisted himself onto it, making his painful way down the length of the bedroom to the far closet. He opened the door, balancing his full weight on one hip, and I shut my eyes. If he fell, he would fall. He would be furious if I tried to help him.

He turned and held it out to me, a soft pile of sable, a tangle of little skins that rippled like liquid when he shook it out. He reminded me of a salesman in an expensive fur salon.

"It was my wife's coat," he said, regarding it impassively. "I suppose I should have done something with it long ago. I'd like you to have it. It looks like a fit."

I got up and took it from him, preening in it in the mirror, calling out delightedly how beautiful it was, what a perfect fit, and all the time the knowledge that he was going to die was stuck somewhere in the back of my throat. Robert knew it, and now I knew it. There would be no second opinion, no consultation. Only I was still ready to fight, refusing to believe. Always the last to accept to let go, to admit I must do without.

The August sun was beating down on my bare head, and I felt a little lightheaded. Over the heads of the next of kin, I could see the bearers withdrawing, and I knew Robert would have felt they were suitable, quite a decent show. Newbury's always does it right. And now the minister was motioning to us that it was over. We were like guests who didn't know when to leave the party.

We turned away, the little group of us, the elderly gentlemen in their tropical worsteds and their club ties offering their arms to the ladies Robert had left behind him. Not many of either; not many had outlived him. I didn't know who they were. I didn't know about all of Robert's life, just a small piece of it and what he cared for me to know.

I walked past the long funeral limousines, the line of decent black opulence, to my little white Ford at the end of the line. There were just three private cars, mine and two others, and I wondered who had driven them here in the August heat at the tag end of this cortege.

Going over the bridge from the cemetery, I tried to think of something funny. My ancient aunt once told me that one makes jokes on the way to and from the cemetery. She didn't tell me why, because she could see I was far too young, but I know now that it is so you won't notice that the corpse they are burying is really you. And I thought that the joke was this time on me, because I was the one left and now I would have no one in the world to whom I would be sending a Valentine.

All the way down to *Wilderness Ways* I hoped Evan would be there. I looked at my watch when I got out of the elevator, and saw to my disappointment that it was only eleven o'clock. I wanted very much to talk to somebody, and he seemed like a likely person. Turning the corridor, I realized that I was going to be very disappointed if he wasn't there.

He was there, hunched over a mishmash of photographs, reference books and correspondence, and when he looked up and saw me, he actually smiled. It was especially flattering because it didn't take much clairvoyance to see that his face was not accustomed to a smile.

He reached out his hand for the work and gave it a casual glance, lifting the first page absently and then tossing it to the top of the pile.

"Lunch?" he said.

"At eleven?"

"Well, elevenses, then," he said. "Something. I've

been hoping you'd be down soon."

He reached with one long arm for his jacket on the back of the door, took my elbow and propelled me toward the door. All the way down in the elevator he appeared to be thinking about something else, and it wasn't until we emerged into the searing oven of the avenue that he even looked at me. Not until we were waiting for a light at a cross street did he speak.

"You took longer than usual with the job this time," he said, peering down at me.

It wasn't an accusation of complaint, just a statement of fact, and I knew it.

"A friend died," I said, and his face clouded with concern.

"Somebody close?"

I nodded. Too complicated a story. A car was coming down the avenue, one fender flapping noisily, its paint all ruined and the injury overlaid with huge letters saying Ouch. That's me, that car, I said silently. Accident victims both.

He did not press it, and we walked the rest of the way to Gino's in silence.

What a strange man this was, with his unapologetic silences, his sudden metamorphosis from disinterested employer to luncheon companion, his total lack of need for social badinage and his bald assumption that I would not care. Even when he spoke, it was largely words with question marks after them. The habit of reporting had left its mark on his conversation, making me feel interrogated, like the bystander who has happened to be on the scene when the event took place. Yet the way to his own private center was clearly mined with fierce bastions of defense.

Over the Dubonnet he wondered politely again about my friend.

"Robert?" I said. "Robert was a legacy from my husband. He will leave a hole, and my life is already too full of holes. You can hold it up to the light and see that the fabric is sieved. I seem to get the feeling that everybody is dying on me. Robert was the latest."

He considered this. "Not a love affair?"

I had to smile. "Hardly. Just someone who in some strange way I loved. It's not at all the same, you know."

Do you promise to love me always and never let anyone or anything come between us ever? That kind of thing is over. Toward the end you have to settle for bits and pieces, like the salt tack and crackers you manage to salvage for the raft after a shipwreck. Maybe you can put together Robert love and Katie love, and anything else you can find to scrape together and make do. Comfortable bits and pieces for deprived folks.

He had been studying me again.

"Actually I *don't* know," he said. "I got lost early. A marriage that didn't work out and that I kept holding onto because there wasn't anything better around and because of the kids. When they were passing out the real thing, I was absent from school. But it's impossible to tell the genuine article from the fraud in the beginning."

All of which accounted for the melancholy, brooding look.

"But you didn't ever try again?" I said incredulously. I couldn't believe it. A man in his early sixties, a nice, decent man, and any man at all gets a lot of shots at the brass ring. We all know that. Perhaps I should tell him about the Matchmaker.

The wintry smile made a brief appearance and disappeared. "Oh, I tried plenty of times while I was still married," he said. "That turned out to be a mistake, too. Not the kind of image for a father, so I lost the children, too. Who can blame them? Now I'm just the guy who sends the alimony check."

"I'm sorry," I said, and I really was. People get lost in all kinds of different ways. It takes one to know one.

"Still," I said, "I can't somehow seem to envision you wasting away in a lonely garret."

He was beckoning the waiter. "What?" he said. I had hit the bad left ear.

The hamburgs came, terribly overdone, but it was somehow nice to be sitting there with someone who had also discovered that life doesn't offer any guaranteed storybook endings. We ate thoughtfully, contemplating the heat outside the window and our own problems.

"What God-awful food this is," he said when he put down his fork. "When you come in next, we'll order in wine and cheese and picnic."

It was somehow nice to hear him talk about when I came in next.

Chapter 22

"I THINK," I said to Alexia, "I will have a face-lift. I am tired of looking in the mirror and seeing my mother. Just a little tuck here and a little lift there and I could slip back ten years. Drive men mad."

Alexia and I share the same birth year, but a capricious fate awarded to her the kind of patrician features that don't seem to be affected by the laws of gravity. I don't remember seeing all these lines arching down from nose, mouth and throat almost three years ago when I was just a housewife wondering what to serve for dinner. I keep pinching things up to see how I would look, smooth skinned and slightly Chinese-looking with uptilted eyes, but I know it is in the same class with trying on your mother's dress when you're little, only reverse. Sometimes I think if I had the money, I would let the surgeon's knife erase everything that has happened to me in the last couple of decades, but almost always I know I probably wouldn't. I've looked a lot of reality in the eye since then, and aging might as well get in line with the rest.

Alexia didn't even bother to remind me that we had both seen Harriet after she had had a face-lift, before the swelling went down. She looked as if she had been assaulted.

"Your daughter is your compensation for being no longer young," said Alexia in one of her infrequently mealymouthed pronouncements. "You've had your turn."

Huh. I was not quite ready to sit down and watch the show from the back row. That's how I happened to tell her about Evan.

There wasn't much to tell, but it certainly got her attention. Was I considering, ah, anything serious, anything that would change my life? Evan and I had had two lunches and she was the mother of a debutante daughter. I regretted opening my mouth.

I did not mention Evan to Joan or to Ted. Meetings with unattached males are not what children want to hear from their mother. I especially never report to them when an occasional single male is invited to dinner to balance the table with me. It hardly ever happens, anyway, and when it does, nothing ever comes of it except that I go home with a perverse sense of having failed my hostess. I feel a strong obligation to captivate, to sparkle, to dazzle this rare unattached man she has laid before me generously like a game trophy. In this way I have been introduced to a Jesuit priest, a man with three divorced wives and a Polish embassy attaché

whose English was nearly as bad as my Polish.
Led forward by the hand in this way by my friends, I am recalcitrant. Something in it always puts me off. I feel, at the age of fifty-nine, like a young girl at her first country-club dance, whose parents hover on the sidelines hoping partners will cut in.
"Elizabeth plays golf very well," they will murmur, or, "Elizabeth writes." The stranger and I eye each other over the rim of a glass, smile and turn away.

All this, as I have said, happens very rarely. Single male dinner partners in their fifties are five times more scarce than unattached women, and what happens in the sixties doesn't bear thinking about. Men who have attained this age with any degree of success don't want to spend the evening with women who can match their years. And they don't have to.

Above all, of course, all the world loves a widower. So tragic, left behind so helpless—married and single women alike vie to smooth his path. Who cooks for him? Who runs that house that Mae kept so spotless for thirty years? Women rally around clucking.

Over the roses in her backyard, my neighbor, Sarah, told me about a widowed friend who lost his wife at sixty, ending a Héloïse-and-Abelard love affair that had endured for more than thirty years. Sarah and his other friends feared that he might grieve to a point that could mean a serious decline. When such a marriage is suddenly all over, one hardly knows what to say. His future was much discussed; kind invitations were constantly issued. Sarah had been out of town at the time of the death, and when two months later she saw him at a party, she bypassed the usual social kiss to put both arms around him in a bear hug that she hoped spoke volumes about sad loss and doomed love.

When he could untangle her arm, he drew forward the young girl who was standing next to him.

"Sarah," he said, smiling proudly, "I want you to meet my wife."

"Christ," said Bill, Sarah's husband, on the way home in the car, "when I think how I struggled over the condolence letter."

Joan lives alone in a trailer in a small Georgia town, and even the sound of the telephone when I call down there has a lonesome ring. It sounds different from when I call Alexia or Harriet or Ruth, hollower and tinnier, and I imagine I can hear the relays kicking in all the way down there—Roanoke, Charlotte, Greensboro, Atlanta, and then the two rings for the country phone that One Ring and Three Ring sometimes pick up if things are dull.

Does she find it too lonesome? How does she cope with a strange Southern town where girls do not leave home until they marry and, as she has already observed, do not think life possible without a man in it, do not plan any real alternative to the altar and the bassinet. Probably at twenty-four you know that this is simply a pit stop on the road to success, that farther on are bright lights and people who will want to hold your hand, ask where you have been, love you.

Joan is spartan, so I never really know the low points of her life, everything being edited so as not to lean. In return I try not to be the Spanish Inquisition, so that often the way I learn about her life is to be present when she's telling someone else about it. In these moments I affect elaborate disinterest while a whole door swings wide and, for a little while at least, I understand that many of my notions of life are passé.

Nicest of all is when she brings her friends, whose mother I am not, so that through them I am privy to things Joan does not tell me. When she visits we ask in her friends and, being the cook, I am allowed to listen later to the postprandial talk.

On the evening I am thinking of, they were inquiring about life in the intriguing hinterlands, about which they knew so little. All had entertained vague notions at one time or another of trying such a life, though none had done so. They wondered if she had met any men.

"Anybody interesting, I mean," qualified Lucy, curled on the sofa with her feet tucked under her, fashionable, terrible clodhopper shoes neatly paired on the rug beneath, her blond hair falling across her face.

Joan considered this. "Not really," she said. From the way she said it, I knew Ian had faded into the backdrop.

"I don't suppose it's like here, where everybody is working pro bono and you can go to the same meetings and know everybody else," ventured Allan.

No, said Joan, it was not, shaking her head earnestly. She is entirely different with her friends than with me, very subtly altered, a self-assured, internally lit female who appears to know exactly what she wants. I feel, looking at her, as if I am watching a play, sitting in the dark, removed from the action, allowed to stay up beyond my bedtime, which was indeed some time ago. Whatever restraint a mother's presence exerts was overbalanced by a preponderance of friends. I was looking at a stranger with a family resemblance to my daughter.

"It was hard at first," she said, looking back by way of her wineglass, "but I went into the nearby university town and had a beer in the local place. You pick up people that way."

She looked at Allan as if she were explaining the tribal

habits of a faraway country which he could have no possible way of knowing about, Female kindly explaining to Male. I kept very quiet so they wouldn't notice me.

"Getting to know people is better since it's okay to call men," said Wendy, who is wearing a fetching floor-length African dhobi and a hand-painted vest. "I feel very comfortable now about asking for somebody's telephone number, saying I'll call."

General murmurs of agreement. During the past two years, it seems, the last social taboo has fallen without my knowing it. Nobody need wait by the telephone any longer. Loneliness is dead. Allan agrees, and so does Dick. These pretty young women carry black books and small stubby pencils and have no qualms about stepping up to a likely-looking man and suggesting a subsequent meeting. Women have been picking men for decades, but always before we had to pretend. We included the object of our interest in a large party, or we asked a friend to introduce us, or we stumbled upon him quite by chance, in a pig's eye, at a hockey game. And now all this devious behavior was clearly unnecessary. The millenium had arrived without me knowing. The simplicity of it all was blinding.

But what about rejection? Loss of face? Undermining of self-esteem? Failure and inferiority complex?

I couldn't stand it any longer.

"But what," I cried, forgetting my low profile, "if they don't like your looks?"

They laughed confidently. And indeed who would not like their looks, such doe-eyed, intelligent, willowy creatures? Trauma of this kind was clearly not a threat; it was behind them, discarded like a cocoon. Once they may have been tentative, but all this was over. What young man could possibly resist being chosen by these self-assured young Amazons with their meaningful jobs, their flowing hair and their familiarity with all secrets necessary to know when you are young and female?

"Well, of course," said Lucy, smiling devastatingly, "if they mutter they can't quite remember their new number, they've just moved, or their week looks tight, how about next week, then of course you get the message." She spread her hands palms up and figuratively tossed aside such rejections as unimportant, part of a game, which was after all only a game.

The lovely thing about raising daughters is that one way or another you find out how it is.

I was born in the wrong generation.

Monday morning, alone again and lonely, I picked up the telephone.

"Hello," I said, very throwaway as I had been taught. "I haven't finished the piece yet, but I feel in need of a break. Should we lunch?"

"Absolutely," he said, in his hoarse vulture voice. "What time will you be here?"

Lucy, Wendy, it was easy. And it makes you feel so good. You must come to our house more often.

We were sitting on the floor of Evan's office, dining on a long hunk of French bread, a slab of Port du Salut and a cheap bottle of wine. The sunshine reached around the corner of the building and fingered the cobwebs attached to the venetian blind in the window. It was the right kind of place for Evan, suitable somehow, unfancy but adequate, removed from the world.

"It's a nice wine," I said. We were drinking it from the paper cups from the water cooler, which imparted a cardboard taste that didn't improve it.

"No, it's not," he said, staring at it as if he were wondering how it got into his hand. "It's just cheap. You don't mind, do you?"

I didn't mind anything. I didn't mind the fact that my stockings were probably going to run, or that this was another quite inadequate window air conditioner unable to cope, or that I had a suspicion I was coming down with a late summer cold. It was just companionable, sitting there and looking at him munching off a heel of bread, with the door shut to show that he was off duty and couldn't be consulted on problems.

"When you were a little boy," I began and it seemed suddenly perfectly all right for me to think about his being a little boy, "did you picnic like this on the banks of some river, and fish, and hang out with the barn cats and have an idyllic sort of Currier-and-Ives life?"

"Never picnics like this. And none of the other, really. My father was the publisher of a small-town paper, a country weekly. He wanted to pass it all on to me. I was only about ten when I went down with him to be a copyboy summers. He loved that paper better than my mother. He spent all his time there, a lot of it teaching me how to run it."

"What happened then?"

"He died. And she couldn't sell it quick enough. I guess it was kind of her rival."

"Did you have brothers and sisters?"

"No. I was a lonely small boy."

It was somehow very reassuring to find that he knew about loneliness, and I told him about my cousin, who was married five times and ended up finally so alone that she longed even for junk mail.

"She was very pretty," I said, helping myself to

another bit of wine, "and everybody fell in love with her, but somehow nothing really worked out."

He brushed crumbs off his untidy tweed legs.

"It happens a lot," he said. "Why don't we take a walk?" He unfolded himself and gave me a hand up.

We walked past the receptionist and into the elevator and into the heat of the street, turning north on the avenue, where the traffic was knotted into an immobile snarl punctuated by angry taxi drivers. We crossed the street and strolled along in the early September sunshine until we reached the park, where the old men were playing chess and the winos were sprawled on the benches among the pigeons, drifting in their own private world. On the edge of the fountain someone was playing a mandolin, and the big clock over the bank said it was two o'clock, late for lunch hour for somebody responsible for the entire publication of *Wilderness Ways*, bimonthly and due soon. But we kept walking.

"If you like to walk," he said after a while, "we could walk in the country."

I thought how very nice it would be to walk in the country without first taking off my engagement ring and my watch in case I was mugged, and without having to worry about that strange-looking man approaching from the other direction who might or might not be a simple hiker. Or wondering if I should carry a little cash so as not to irritate anybody who attacked me by turning out to be penniless.

"I'd like that," I said, and he reached down and took my hand to guide me through the traffic madness of the street we were crossing. And all the way back he never let go of it, so we strolled along together, two middle-aged people, flattening our noses against the windows displaying designer jeans and love potions, devices to wear after corrective surgery and flower arrangements, Cuisinarts and the latest best-sellers, all the junk and useless delights that money can buy on the main streets of New York.

When we came to the window of the office-equipment firm underneath his office, he stopped a moment and appeared to be staring at the file cabinets with Slashed Prices, Less Than Half Price.

"It was nice," he said and turned away and went up the stairs to his office.

Chapter 23

We were having lunch, Louis and I, in a new restaurant on East Fifty-eighth, a very elegant restaurant evoking the finest in Rome. Louis delights in discovering the very best wherever it may be, the newest, the most expensive, the posh. Where did you get that word, Ted asked me once, I never hear it from anyone but you. Can it be that I am the last survivor of the ocean-liner era, when the desirable sunny side of the ship for the deck chair was Port Out, Starboard Home?

I had almost forgotten about such restaurants. Fresh white truffles over the finest plume veal, crisp green salad with a delicate dressing, tartuffo ice cream laced with Grand Marnier and decorated with bitter chocolate. "Which dessert would you choose," I could hear Joan saying in my ear not so long ago, "if we were rich?"

"I love New York," Louis was saying, gazing benevolently at his beef carpaccio. "So vibrant and so full of everything one could possibly want. I don't even mind the trash in the streets and the Texas ten-gallon hats. It's part of the package. Sometimes I wonder what I'm doing out there in Putnam County."

Everything was so civilized and reassuring. In Louis's company, I always feel more easy. Just looking at his elegant tailoring, the calm assurance he projects, I knew that my difficulties would recede, money would accrue, love would once more find me. The apprehension that dogged my midnight insomniac hours melted away as I sat across from Louis in this elegant room. I sipped my wine and felt briefly no longer vulnerable.

He looked well, fit; and I told him so. He preened, reached like a child into his briefcase for his clippings. He had been pushing the book everywhere, the demand was good, he had found the lecture tour, the talk shows to his liking, as I had always known he would. Polished, urbane, he had captivated his audiences, laid the mantle of erudition on basic urges offered elsewhere with a snigger. He was doing the only thing in the world that really mattered to him; his mission was beautifully clear. I envied him. Our partnership seemed distant as the Ice Age, but some pleasant residue remained.

Over the wine he inspected me covertly.

"You look different," he said. "Or no, you *seem* different. Less struggling."

"I hope not," I said, eyes on the tray of out-of-season strawberries being wheeled past. They rose, berry on berry, to a magnificent pyramid. "I need to struggle. Maybe I like myself better, or maybe I just make more allowances. I'm not making many value judgments these days."

I picked up a lot of jargon from having children who were adolescent in the sixties.

"You've met someone," Louis said, putting down his wineglass and smiling triumphantly. "That's it. That's the explanation. I'm right, am I not?"

"Not really," I said.

On top of the sixties I had graduate courses from Joan's friends on how never to make a positive statement.

"Sexual affair?" His eyes were sparkling.

"Louis, you dirty old man," I said without rancour. "These days my orgies take place in my dreams and usually consist of letting someone put sugar in my tea when I know I gave it up a long time ago."

He looked disconsolately at the salad on his plate.

"I'm disappointed," he said. "A nice girl like you ought to have plenty of offers. I'd make one myself, if I thought you'd accept, but I don't think you would. I hate it when people get the idea that sex is over with youth."

"Who gets the idea?" I replied, stung. "And who says I haven't had offers?"

Louis pushed the salad ever so slightly to one side and lit a Marlboro. It always amuses me, the image of Louis the Marlboro man astride the horse, galloping tall in the saddle in pursuit of man's work on the plains.

"I knew it," he said, looking genuinely delighted. "Good."

I opened my mouth to deny it, as I had once wanted to tell the Safeway clerk I had got back too much change. But the world was topsy-turvy and I was a different person, and if Louis chose to believe that I was in the midst of a love affair, then why not let him. It gave him pleasure. I said nothing at all.

"One of the nice things about getting older," he said, "is that you no longer have to account to anybody else. You don't hurt anybody, because nobody cares."

No, nobody cares. Not Judith, who has made a life elsewhere. Not Booth, who is dead. Not anybody at all, except possibly out of curiosity. But I care.

What I cared about was the realization that I was sitting opposite Louis, allowing him to dress me up in the appearance of an affair which, thirty-five years ago when I was actually conducting one, I would have done anything to conceal. It was Alice down the rabbit hole again, and I would surely never survive playing with such rules. We were playing croquet with flamingos for mallets and hedgehogs for balls, and I was pretending that it was all quite normal. But then something had to be done to spike Louis's image of me as a brave, resourceful Brontë heroine.

"The tartuffo?" Louis invited, blowing Marlboro circles in the air.

"Yes, I guess so," I said. If only for Joan.

Evan and I walked the countryside. Fall that year was not so much an explosion of color as a gradual drying up. The frost was late and the days were golden, a light reprise of summer's heat without the pain. We walked the deserted beaches toward the tip of Long Island, flushing the shore birds as we made lonely footprints in the sand. Sometimes we left the sea and drove up the river, parking the car like an outpost base and striking out into wood-bordered pastureland.

I walked briskly and he loped, which kept us in some sort of accommodation. We brought sandwiches and wine and sat on fallen logs to eat and drink while we watched the leaves reassort themselves with every breath of air.

We avoided, by mutual unspoken consent, talk of anything that had gone before. We drifted, without past or future, like the leaves we watched in the river. I knew that he was paying a good deal of alimony, that his son refused to speak to him; he knew that I was a widow of going on three years. Beyond that, very little. Sometimes I thought perhaps the middle-aged man was as lonely as the small boy in New Hampshire had been, but he never really said so, though once he came close.

He was lying on his back on a fallen tree, eyes tight shut, apparently asleep.

"It's better since I knew you," he said. And that was all.

"I saw you coming out of an office building with a nice-looking tall, thin man," said Harriet, giving me her provocative smile. "Is it someone who would make a nice fourth for bridge?"

"No. I got him at the Matchmaker Computer Dating Center and it said right on his form that he hated cards. Collecting butterflies and belly dancing are his main interests."

"Ever the card," said Harriet, giving me an uncertain look because, after all, it could be true. "Do you want to bring him to dinner or anything?"

"No, mother." Somehow it seemed better if Evan and I kept our friendship in limbo.

"He must eat with the wrong fork," said Harriet, who loves to meet new men. "Or are you afraid of the competition?"

"It's just a rather tenuous friendship, that's all."

It wasn't really a tenuous friendship, just a friendship with limits. We wandered through the art galleries together, stomped through the rain in the cold countryside. Once in a while we got into his ancient, unreliable Fiat and drove to some inn for lunch, sitting in front of the fire, sipping our coffee, comfortable with each other. Yet there were days at a time when we didn't see each other, days when I imagined he was holed up with the Great American Novel in his West Side apartment, but I felt no lack. I never saw that apartment and I never wanted to. And like a girl seeing a man of whom her parents would not approve, I never brought him back to my house. He didn't belong in that house; he wasn't part of that life. He was somebody to keep me from being alone, somebody to do things with, not to bring home.

He would depart my life for almost a week, and then the phone would ring.

"Everything okay?" he would ask, and his voice always made it sound as if he really wanted to know. "I thought we might go to Gino's tonight. Is that all right?"

As if we had already planned to meet and it was only a question of where.

He knew a good deal about art and hardly anything at all about anything published since 1850, unless it had to do with animals. He had a taste for the classics and a child's preferences in food, caring almost nothing about what went into his mouth. He had never read a comic strip until we met and listened with interest when I explained Snoopy to him. He read three newspapers a day, studying them seriously like an Oriental puzzle. Like most big men, he was gentle and generous.

"What about this man?" said Alexia, "the one you mentioned. Has he dropped out of sight? You never speak of him."

"I see him occasionally," I said. "I think maybe he's lonely, like me. In an odd sort of way. Has it ever occurred to you that one day you will be physically crushed by the silence in your house?"

It is inconceivable that Alexia should admit such a weakness, even if it were so.

"I'm so busy with lawyers and insurance and the will," she said. "So busy I guess I don't notice. I thought you had it licked."

"I never said that."

It was strange that even with Evan added to my life, it wasn't really very much better. I had longed for a man to take me to dinner, and now I had one. Yet every morning I was opening my eyes on a day that held no real promise, only more of the same. The world outside my window seemed to offer only obligations and struggle. Nothing truly hurt anymore. What I had was absence of pain.

Stirring my tea at Alexia's pretty table, I was ashamed. Very few people get beyond some sort of compromise with life.

The underlying ache was permanent, though small things could divert me. Let me find my little gold watch, I said very clearly to God a few weeks ago; let me find it and I will brace up and be grateful for what I have. The little gold watch was very dear to me, a present from Booth on my birthday. Half the night I was searching the backyard with a flashlight, peering down the disposal, sorting through the trash, retracing footsteps from the day's peregrinations. I went to bed praying wordlessly for its return, and the next morning I arose and went straight to the birthday present I was wrapping for Joan and found it caught in the tissue paper.

If that isn't answered prayers, I don't know what is. And an hour later, watch back on my wrist, I was complaining to myself that with no one to talk to, I was becoming a solo mutterer.

Alexia was looking at me sharply.
"Would you have an idea of marrying again?"
I laughed.
"The only man I'm seeing I can't bring myself to invite to the house."

Thanksgiving is one of those days you have to have family around. They are supposed to come, wherever they may be, clogging the train stations and the airports and the highways en route home to the family condominium. Next to Christmas, it is the worst day in the year to be alone, to admit that in the whole world, although you have friends, you don't have priority with someone. Anybody who has to can stumble through New Year's Eve alone, but Thanksgiving has all those connotations of large tables, loving holiday baking of breads and pies, closeness, a Norman Rockwell sort of scene with the family tight against the world.

Joan was coming home, but Ted was not. At the old walnut table with the claw feet where we had eaten so many meals as four, there would be too many empty chairs. The contrast between the Now and the Then would choke us both as we tried to be thankful for the bird and the cranberry sauce. I ran over all the people in my mind who might be lonely on Thanksgiving, and Evan kept intruding.

But surely he would be going back to New Hampshire, no doubt to an invalid mother, lingering on only for a glimpse of her son. I could see the snowy scene in my mind, a cutter, perhaps, Evan with the robe over hs knees, urging on the horses, and a wrinkled face framed in a bonnet peering expectantly from a snow-drifted window at the end of the driveway. He would lope up the steps and enfold her in his arms. Did he love her? He never spoke of her. It is required to love your mother, but not everybody does.

"Will you be going back to New Hampshire for Thanksgiving?" I inquired, basking in front of the fire beside him at a little inn in Garrison. "Your mother still live there?"

He turned to look at me.

"My mother's dead. Has been for ten years."

Pause, as he refilled my cup and his from the pot by the fireplace.

"Your daughter coming?" he said, stirring his cup with enormous attention.

"I think so."

In the secret garden of my heart, I didn't want to ask him for Thanksgiving. I wanted to want to, but I didn't. Ask him, I ordered myself impatiently, but the words wouldn't come. The scene *à trois* would be doomed from the start, a shipwreck to be avoided.

"I think we're going to a friend's," I lied and left it there. Sometimes I don't like myself very much.

In the end I asked Josie's husband, Edward, because he would be alone. Josie was visiting in Europe. Edward loves Joan, probably because she is a friend of his daughter and Edward is besotted with his daughter, who was also not coming home. And so we three found ourselves a make-do little group, thrown together by chance and a certain amount of deprivation, speaking often of the people who weren't at the table, tied together by familiarity and years of shared meals, car pools and visits back and forth.

Joan and I had spared no effort, stuffing the turkey with chestnuts, oysters and celery, making cranberry bread, sweet-potato soufflé, a pecan pie, choosing a wine that none of us had the palate to appreciate. We got down the big silver platter and ringed it with parsley bouquets, stood on tiptoe to get down the party dishes, bought pink chrysanthemums for the Chinese bowl.

I hadn't thought of saying grace. I think perhaps I am agnostic, except when I'm scared, and then I do my praying without benefit of words, let alone ritual ones. But Edward is a deeply religious man and he asked if he might say it.

I didn't want him to do it. I didn't feel particularly thankful, and it seemed all wrong. Too many empty chairs. Best to gloss over things, look away from the holes, not turn down the empty glass.

But Edward, uncomplicated Edward, was reaching for my hand and across the table for Joan's, and it was too late. Joined by our hands, we bowed our heads, and he murmured the old prayer over us.

Edward speaks with deliberation, and I had time to think. Not of Booth, because that is always there at such moments like the foundation under the floor, but of Ted and what he might be doing at this moment.

And just before the Amen, I wondered if Evan was making his dinner out of a can somewhere over on the West Side.

Chapter 24

It couldn't happen, not a major snowstorm before Christmas, but it had. I opened my window on the beautiful, quiet white blanket I remember from my childhood in upstate New York, lace on the hemlocks in the back, the whole street pristine, unmarked by footprints, including those of the paper boy.

I opened the door wide for Katie, who for once would be in no danger of being run over. She stood poised for a moment on the doorstep, a black exclamation point in a white world, and then took the steps in a single bound to wade into it, biting great mouthfuls and tossing it like a ball into the air. I watched her joyous progress, a Landseer dog in a Currier and Ives scene, and shut the door on the biting wind.

Now the boots, so I could refill the bird feeder. Ancient Frieda went with me, stepping high and surprised by what she felt underfoot. The sparrow who obviously lives in the stove exhaust vent winter or summer was waiting patiently in the bush nearby, and the cardinal kept watch from the tangle of wisteria on the fence, awaiting his turn. A bit of horse meat for each dog and a poached egg for me, and what to do with the rest of the day?

Walks take precedence over everything except death, and Frieda and I set forth as usual, explorers in a new world, all familiar smells covered, the curbs by which she measures the distance with an exploratory paw obliterated. Ringed around by the circles of foolish Kate, enduring the playful little darts and bites, she stepped along with dignity, spavined as Don Quixote's horse, a dog that had seen snows come and go and would outlast this one, too.

Above our heads the neighbors' shades remained drawn, windows still cracked for the night's fresh air. It was Sunday, a Sunday in spades, a day when everything had come to a complete halt. My little car stood patiently at the curb, its roof and hood bowed by more than a foot of snow. When and if the plow came through, its path to the Safeway, the post office, the bank and *Wilderness Ways* would be blocked by the drifts shoved against it from the center of the road.

At the end of the street, a wisp of smoke was already threading through the chimney of another early riser. I too could have a cozy fire, the kind the day demanded, a cheerful blaze to warm us by. In nearly three years I had learned how to build a good fire. The dogs would be delighted, plumping themselves down as near as possible without actually roasting their hides. Is it worth building a fire for just dogs? Or just for me?

Ever since I closed the door behind us, I had been thinking of Robert, in his grave above his wife out in the cemetery, since space in cemeteries, as elsewhere, is at a premium. Robert did so love heat; his apartment was always breathlessly close. And of all people, Robert liked someone to pass the time of day with. At the very last he had told one of his nurses that he supposed conversation between him and his wife would be difficult in the grave, like a conversation between occupants of a Pullman upper and lower.

I took a deep, icy breath. Robert is gone and so is Booth, and I am left holding the bag with the future. Keep busy, push down the used-to-be. Today, I decided, plodding behind Frieda, I shall metamorphosize into the quintessential housewife, make cookies, wax the floors, polish the furniture. It is a day for shining up the homestead, for caretaking of possessions, for forgetting problem situations.

And I will call Joan.

Joan was asleep.

"It's snowing," I said, anxious to communicate the whiteness and the cold over the tiny wire to Georgia. "I've shoveled a path from the front door to the street, and the snow on each side is higher than Katie's back."

That was nice. Yes, she was well. Conversation with Joan, when she has just waked, is like batting a tennis ball against the garage door: one sided, a game without zest. No, there was no snow there; she would write. I hung up with my need for a brush with humanity unsatisfied.

The shoveling, at any rate, had been fun, if fraught with the usual accompanying scenario of disaster, Katie nosing my inert form in the snow, investigating with a tentative paw as I lay ashen, gasping for oxygen, wondering if her dinner might be delayed. The newspaper had warned against unaccustomed shoveling because cold air plus exertion was hazardous for the aging.

Aging? Hell. I made the snow fly, widening the path a little to thumb my nose at such talk. People at risk were obviously not like me, did not do ten sit-ups every night before going to bed, five leg-overs and ten scissor kicks. A girl who had been stroke on the school crew, a forward wing on the hockey team and captain of the basketball team can surely laugh at shoveling a suburban walk.

Probably.

I went inside and made myself a cup of tea, no sugar, and carried it restlessly through the house. There was something about the snow that chilled me beyond cold, isolated me more than I understood. I was suspended in limbo, the neighbors a mere light across the street, a wisp of smoke, complete in their family circles, phoning the kids to say see you next Sunday, don't think of venturing out. Probably playing backgammon and reading *Snowbound*. I felt discriminated against, depressed, ready to foment a social revolution. I alone was locked up in a house pregnant with the past. I wanted my share of cozy domestic life behind drawn curtains.

Alone in the house and unable to shake off the black mood with a useless errand, everything around me seemed to murmur of happier times. There were the children's diplomas and cum-laude certificates, scorned and left behind by them, still marching in rows down the wall beside the carpeted stairs to the recreation room. There on the china closet full of my grandmother's china was the pink griffin candle I bought for a staggering sum in Spain that summer Booth and I visited Robert. Here on the ledge in the kitchen were the pebbles we four had gathered on our vacation on the beach at Cape Cod. They looked dusty and out of place. Away from the sea they had lost their luster, lost the iridescent shimmer that they had developed consorting with fish. Some of them were once Joan's prizes, but it was I who had found them and sown them in front of her path so that Ted, running far ahead, darting back and forth in his haste to find the treasures of the beach, should not have all the best. I only told her that last year, and her eyes widened in disbelief. Had I once so controlled destiny, tampered with her stars without her knowing?

The day was scarcely half over, and I had a bad case of cabin fever. Frantic to immerse myself in domestic duties, I gathered up the trash and took it down through the garage to the snow-capped trashcans outside. No one would come to pick it up, but no matter, chores were comforting, steadied the uneasy restlessness. Wash a load of clothes, run it through the dryer, fold everything neatly and put it away in the linen closet. Valium is nothing to the soothing power of folding and putting away clean linen in orderly piles on shelves.

What better time to try on skirts to check hemlines? One by one I jerked them from the closet, slipped them over my head and regarded myself in the mirror. Too short, unbecoming, this pile, that pile. Only a few made it back into the closet, accepted, a neat row of the chosen in which I need not feel apologetic.

Close the door on them, on the glimpse of my mother's evening dress hanging on the pink padded satin hanger, on a shirt of Booth's that somehow missed the great giveaway. How things do outlast people, how eloquently they speak of them from dark closets, retain the shape and lingering scent of people long after the owners are gone. Patiently they await any attention, however slight, however infrequent, requiring nothing, keepers of the past. Two New Year's Eves ago I wore my mother's black net evening gown to a party at Alexia's. I sat quite still on her best chair, shedding paillettes like a molting canary, careful not to strain the brittle material. My mother did the Charleston in that dress.

I took it down, holding it against me in the mirror. My mother was prettier than I; all the pictures say so. And never as old as I am today. In this dress she was young.

I put the dress back in the closet and studied myself in the mirror. How had I looked in that dress that New Year's Eve? What I saw in my reflection did not reassure me. Gravity and things I didn't care to think of had affected the contours of my face, written their signatures and the whole story relentlessly. What made me tell Louis—or allow him to think—that men had made advances to me? It could only be his familiar total obsession with the eternal life of sex that made him imagine such things happen to middle-aged women.

I had the living proof. Why hadn't Evan propositioned me?

A friend is someone whose telephone number you know without looking it up. On that basis I have four and a half friends, the half being a close acquaintance whose telephone number is a cinch to remember. I get telephonitis when the lights begin to come on and there is nobody coming home to tell me how the day went.

"Are you there?" I said to Harriet. "Is there life across the avenue? What are you *doing?*"

"Joe's working in his shop repairing Artie's bedside table, and I'm balancing my checkbook. After that I'm going to make some soup."

Another tight little island, complete within itself. Harriet also has a son who lives at home and one who lives nearby. Every Sunday cars draw up in front of her house, spilling out family, people who sit around after dinner discussing the hockey team and how to get egg out of tweed trousers, and what a little clicking noise under the hood means when it comes only after the car idles.

"Do you want to mush over by dogsled or something? There'll be lots of soup."

No, thanks. A bit too far and a bit too late in the day. Yes, lunch, certainly this week. In the meantime, go back to your secure and happy life, damnit.

I felt worse when I hung up than I had before I'd called. I was a hermit in an isolated cabin, waiting out the storm, forgotten, solitary, extra. I remember seeing the cabin of a famous hermit, which had been moved to a regional museum in Blue Mountain, New York, in the Adirondacks, and I was struck with the orderly neatness of the tiny cabin, the bunk stretched tight under the bearskin, the washbasin in the neatly hollowed out stump and the geometrically stacked firewood. He had everything he needed close at hand. Except, of course, somebody to talk to.

All right, nobody to talk to, how about somebody to talk *at* me? The man on the radio was saying in a rich, ripe voice that there were severe storm warnings for the New York area, travelers' advisory, the meetings of the Victorian Society, the Committee for Mental Health in Babylon, the Hadassah Circle of Huntington were all canceled. His voice was bright and pulsating with controlled excitement. He was bringing the word of the breakdown of communications in the nation's most important city, and he wanted the right people to know.

The hucksters had not taken a holiday. Advertising had a captive audience wondering if they should try to get through to where they had once planned to go. Safeway had a special on regular ground beef, Korvette's Big Pre-Holiday Spectacular with Slashed Prices would extend a full Extra Day because of weather conditions. A Bargain Bonus Day Not To Be Missed. The announcer's voice had become familiar, intimate, folksy.

I snapped it off. It was not a human voice.

It is well known that obstetricians can count on a small surge of births following the proper number of months after a blackout or a snowstorm that paralyzes the city. In a torrid August heat spell, people need space about them; being alone is possible, even desirable. Snow drifting down steadily brings with it the need for human closeness. The lack I felt was like an ache that no aspirin could touch.

I could bear it no longer. I found the local directory and called neighbors. I am building a fire, I said, and I want company. Please come. Come and sip something with me, talk to me to prove that I am.

They came, bringing with them the snow from the porch, stomping their boots apologetically onto the mat, asking where to put them as they stood, stocking-footed, in the hall, laughing and stuffing gloves into their pockets. They brought the outdoors in, made the room small again, reporting on thermometer readings, weather prognostications. Emily, Sarah, Bill, the colonel and his wife, it was like a party. Katie had to be tied to the piano leg, ice had to be gotten out, once more I was part of something. Outside the window the snowflakes were thickening, but now it was all right. We sat on the floor

Chapter 25

WE WERE sitting on one of the benches in the Museum of Modern Art, resting our feet after wandering aimlessly through the rooms. One, two, three, we sat, me and Evan and one of those old ladies with shopping bags and umbrellas who kill their days in public buildings, simply existing until time to go home and make dinner alone on the hot plate in the kitchenette. Evan was staring straight ahead as if he were studying the Picasso still life on the wall opposite, but I had a feeling he wasn't even seeing it.

"Do you like it?" I said, to test. "Including the dead fish?"

"Like what?"

I laughed.

"Actually," he said, "I was thinking about you. I was wondering what you wanted out of life."

"More money from *Wilderness Ways*," I said, but he pretended not to hear me. Maybe he didn't. I had his left ear.

"I mean if you had enough money, would you be happy? Would that be enough? What would you think about then?"

It gave me a strange feeling to hear him talking about things like that. The old lady shuffled her run-down shoes and looked away, but I knew she was listening.

"I don't know, really," I said. "I'd love to find out. I wouldn't be the way I was before, I know that."

"How was that?" he said, still studying the Picasso. "I didn't know you then."

"Mindlessly content. Living life vicariously through the kids and shining up the house. And, of course, I couldn't go back to being part of a pair. So it would never be like that again."

He was silent for so long that the old lady gave up and moved on, shuffling off past the guard, one stocking hanging in folds around her veined leg.

"So what then?" he said after a while. "What would you be like?"

"You mean if I could have whatever I want?"

He nodded.

I thought about it.

"I don't know," I said, floundering about in the idea. "Trying to make money fills so much of my time I don't know what I'd think about if I didn't think about that. Maybe I'd just be terribly at loose ends. I guess I'd like not to be so much alone. Maybe I'd take one of those cruises where there's a botanist on board and you study the wild flowers in the Greek Islands. Maybe I'd work passionately for some wildly improbable political candidate. Something that involved people."

"Yes," he said.

"Yes?"

"Yes, I know what you're talking about."

"I worry a little that life is passing me by," I said. "My daughter knows better how to live. She takes time to smell the flowers, and she sings in the shower. I want to do that, too, but I can't even listen to music. It distracts me from lucrative thought."

He smiled at me. He had a wonderful smile, and it was a pity it didn't get to come out more often.

He unfolded his length carefully, rubbing his knee.

"Let's go down to that place you showed me where the fountain runs down the window and eat."

The room was full of bearded young men and long-haired girls in jeans, with a sprinkling of families with babies. We ordered quiche and wine and stared at the water running down the windowpane.

"So now we've arranged my fantasy life, let's order up yours," I said.

"Why, success as a writer, of course," he said. "And to get out of that crummy apartment I have now." He did what on somebody else's face would have been a double take, a double take in half-time. "You've never seen it, have you? It's just as well. It would depress you. As a matter of fact, I've never seen where you live, either, have I?"

I had a feeling that we were entering onto untried ground, and I wasn't sure I was going to like it. I wanted to keep things the way they were, forever maybe, separate and easy, companionably drifting. I looked at his profile and thought with a stab that it was now getting familiar, almost as familiar as Booth's because it was a more recent overlay.

"My house needs painting," I said, "and my dog's impossible. You would get hairs all over you. She has a heart too easily made glad."

"All right," he said. He didn't say that he understood, but he clearly did, and I felt bad about it. I truly loved this rangy, complicated, turned-inward man and I wanted him to be happy. I didn't really know why I didn't want him parking his Fiat in front of the house, knowing where the bottle opener was kept, where the lights turned on. I couldn't think of anything to say.

We finished our quiche and walked out into the pale winter sunshine, standing for a moment on the street to watch an ambulance scream by through the cowering traffic. A Catholic I once knew used to cross himself whenever an ambulance went by, and I've always wondered whether it was a prayer for the poor devil in trouble or a good-luck charm to ward it off himself. Either way it made sense.

We walked hand in hand to the corner where the Fiat was parked, it being Sunday. It looked even more dilapidated and unassuming than usual, reminding me somehow of Frieda. We were en route to the country, and Evan inserted its battered nose into the traffic heading toward Riverside Drive when a light at a cross street stopped us. In the car ahead of us a young girl, taking advantage of the moment, slid close to the driver and melted into a clinch.

We stared at them through the Fiat's dirty windshield while the traffic passed in front of them. The clinch lasted until the light changed, a moment longer really, long enough to cause impatient honks.

We followed them a block before turning west.

"Do they think they invented it?" Evan said under his breath.

I was seeing more and more of him all the time. The lunches were two-hour affairs, the weekends were understood to be ours; we drifted almost by default into closeness. Once in a while, across the table at Gino's, sitting on the broken spring of the Fiat beside him as we drove into the country, I wondered what I was doing. But most of the time all I knew was that I wasn't so lonely anymore. It was lovely to have someone who parked the car, took your hand, ordered the cheap wine, someone just to walk up the street with. The whole dependency thing was rearing its head, and in quiet moments it worried me. But I was tired of fighting my own battles. Leaning was like taking a break in a race where everybody could run faster.

"Elizabeth?"

"Hm?"

We were sitting on newspapers, leaning against the wall of his office, the current picnic spread out before us.

"Are you happy?"

I stared at him.

"What kind of a question is that?" I said. "You can't ask people that."

"I'm not asking people, I'm asking you."

"No," I said, "of course not. Who's happy? Are you, for instance?"

"I don't really expect to be," he said. "But sometimes you give me the impression you are, that you're rich and happy and don't need anything else. I know you're not rich—you told me so—but I wondered if you were happy."

I stopped chewing and swallowed what was left in my

mouth as if it had suddenly turned to cardboard.

"Why do you come around asking me dumb questions like that?" I said, and in spite of myself tears gathered in my eyes. "People shouldn't go around asking other people if they're happy. It's a very personal question." I swallowed with difficulty. "If you must know, I feel like a refugee, one step ahead of the conquering army and they're gaining on me."

He put down his sandwich and came around to put his arms around me. I put my cheek on his scratchy shoulder and wiped my tears with his tie.

"Don't cry," he said, after a while. "You are important to me."

What would Louis have made of such goings-on, the sort of complicated, introspective pas de deux in which we engaged, when things could so easily sort themselves out if we simply fell into bed together? Louis would no doubt smile and mumble some jargon to make it all seem inevitable and sociologically right—stepping neatly around the enormous courage it takes to make compromises, begin new connections when you are no longer young. Can't a man and a woman be friends?

I would have concealed from Louis that Evan hadn't asked me to be anything else.

No matter, that's what I wanted—comfortable friendship with someone highly compatible like him with no strings. I wanted to drift like this forever, having somebody to do things with. Perhaps in time the children could also think of him as a friend. Uncle Evan? Oh, God. No. Evan, then. Maybe we could all go some weekend to Chadds Ford, where we'd been talking of going. One car, separate rooms. There wasn't, as my mother would have said, anything between us. I had left that kind of thing in another life when I had been so happily, so deliriously in love that I hadn't cared who knew that I was conducting a blatant affair with a married man.

The trouble was that Evan seemed to want exactly that, too. And it is all very well to be prepared to reject advances, to murmur gently of still-unresolved sorrows, but what if you don't get a chance to say no?

Perhaps, I thought in rising alarm, no one could ever think of me as an object of desire again. Maybe that was all behind me and I was wasting my time with the nightly exercises to keep a flat stomach and the ridiculous sums I was paying my hairdresser. How had I failed? When did I go—well—old? When the stone-faced clerk behind the counter at the drugstore sold me some aspirin and automatically pushed toward me the signature list for senior-citizen discount, I was unreasonably furious.

I was not yet sixty, I told him icily, and therefore not eligible for discount.

"Geez, lady, sorry," he said and turned away.

At that time my sixtieth birthday was four months off.

A year earlier I would have grabbed that pencil with alacrity and happily perjured myself. All I wanted then was financial survival. Now I wanted more: survival with embellishments. I wanted people to think I looked attractive. I suddenly wanted to deny the march of time, dress it up, pretend it wasn't there. The reports from the front lines are frightening, and they don't tell us everything. It is strange that so few of us panic, at least openly.

When I was married, I felt young, and the distant future when I would be old held no terrors. I would never be as old as Booth; he was the advance scout, the front line of defense. In his wake, I leaned and did not worry. He read the headlines and I read the funnies. He kept me innocent of the dragons lurking out there—right down to his own approaching death. My world was as secure as a fortress as long as he was alive.

"What are you doing lying there?" I cried in terror when I found him fallen by the foot of the stairs to the driveway. "Are you sick?"

I struggled to get him to his feet, but he was too heavy, too inert.

And all the time he was keeping up the masquerade, protecting me from knowledge of the truth.

"Just leave me alone a moment," he said. "I'll be fine." And, lying on his side, unable to move, he lit a damn cigarette.

Even then I didn't understand, didn't know that he was dying.

"What I want for Christmas is a psychiatrist," I said to Katie, who, sensing social intercourse in the offing, went to get her ball. Katie, the farm dog, living in a suburban house; me, former housewife, living in limbo.

All my friends have psychiatrists.

"No, I can't lunch today, it's my day with Dr. Markus," says Harriet, and Josie, and practically everyone I meet. Alexia does not have a psychiatrist, but she is thinking about getting one. It is de rigueur, the indispensable without which nobody thinks she can function. I long to know what happens inside those expensive offices, what pearls are handed out for a dollar a minute, but though they do not exactly keep the rites secret from the uninitiated, they are vague. "He really doesn't tell me anything, he just makes me see where my values lie." Or, "He asks me questions that reveal myself to me."

My hairdresser just says comfortably that her psychiatrist makes her feel good. Together they all make me feel like the single girl who has blundered into a circle of women talking about childbirth.

Naturally, at a dollar a minute, I do not have a psychiatrist. I have thought of offering five dollars for a sample chat, but I doubt I could interest a doctor. Miraculous help and guidance in life's little problems are not for the lower classes. As a result, I frequently call Dorothy, a widowed college friend of mine who lives in Darien. Long distance, I seem to feel, lends truth, perspicacity and the long view.

She doesn't know any of my present friends, and it is close to forty years since we have met. No matter. She likes to hear from me and adores hearing about problems.

"I've met this man," I said in the phone.

That didn't sound like a problem. About that, who could complain? She herself would like to meet somebody, probably a gay.

Well, yes, it is wonderful and it surely fills in the chinks of my life. But all the time that I'm keeping him separate from my former life, holding him at arm's length, I'm wondering why he doesn't seem to be attracted to me.

Dorothy, the psychiatrist, fee, forty-five cents for the first three minutes on the AT&T weekend discount, is good at finding the flaw in murky ambivalence.

"Do *you* want to go to bed with him?" she wants to know.

No. I love him in a very calm, comfortable way, as if we were tourists exploring a walled city together, drawn together by the fact that we happen to have come this way at the same time and do not speak the language of the country. This is not the love I remember, not even a pale country cousin. That love was destiny, inescapable, preordained and inconvenient. This man is nice to have around, like a very dear teddy bear.

The doctor was in.

"Why are you keeping him separate from your friends? Isn't he presentable?"

Sure, I don't know, I just am. But my psychiatrist, standing at the phone in her Darien kitchen, the cat winding around her ankles and begging audibly for dinner, knows why.

"Maybe you don't want to supplant Booth in that house. This, of course, is silly. Ask the nice man to your Christmas party. You still give it, don't you? Take two aspirin and phone me next week."

"Evan," I said in the very offhand way I adopt when I'm nervous, "why don't you come to our Christmas party? Christmas Eve, if you're not going out of town. The children will be there."

We both pretended it wasn't a moment embroidered with fine threads of drama.

Chapter 26

THE THIRD Christmas party the children and I gave alone was smaller than the others. Some of the people who used to come had dropped away. The first Christmas everybody came, making it clear that they cared, that they remembered, pretending that things would carry on as usual. People will always be kind, at least at first. The second Christmas some of them found they would rather stay home on Christmas Eve, and when I counted dirty glasses, I felt a pang. Booth was the charmer; we were the residue. The third Christmas we had gotten used to it and added a few guests who had known only us.

We made such a thing of preparing for this party that it always came as a surprise that it could all be over in a couple of hours. We shined the silver punch bowl that we borrowed from Josie, made countless watercress sandwiches, stuffed cream cheese into dried beef and rolled it, made mixes and dips in every bowl on the shelf. After this we laid the table with the green cloth and worried, as usual, that no one at all would come, would remark later when we bumped into them at the Safeway that they had tried to make it but things had got complicated. And then suddenly the room was bursting with cheerful noises and chatter, jammed and filled with the smell of perfume and tobacco and wine with an overlay of candle grease.

I am always a very good hostess for a few minutes, after which I tend to relax and become a guest at my own party. I wasn't near the door and I didn't see Evan come in. I looked up and caught his eye across the room and at once felt guilt stricken that I hadn't watched for him, a stranger among people who knew each other. He started making his way toward me, holding a glass in one hand, with the other holding his jacket close so as not to take up more room than necessary. He was making slow progress through the tight knots of people. "Excuse me," he said to Emily, and "Excuse me," to Josie, and then he was standing beside me, towering over me and smiling that rare smile.

"Merry Christmas," he said when he kissed me.

"Who was that big rangy fellow who came in toward the last?" inquired Ted as we were cleaning up. "Do I know him?"

Nothing stays the same. Even Christmas changes its face ever so slightly over the years. Only the camera nails down the moment to remind you later, with a pang, of how it was. You think things can stay as they are, it seems so simple, but they never do.

I, too, was changing my face. Clip, clip, clip, my credit card at Lord & Taylor as Booth's wife was dropping piece by piece into the trash in favor of the new one I had requested in my own name. Over in the credit department I was now nobody's wife but just another woman trying to establish credit late in life. I could have wept, mourning myself as I was. The rite symbolized everything I had to leave behind. The credit bureau had explained that paying bills in Booth's name only preserved a dead man's credit.

"It was hard," I told Evan. "Some sort of milestone."

He was staring at a photo of a horseshoe crab being bled for science, trussed up for the sacrifice.

"Yours was a good marriage, wasn't it?" he said, removing his eye from the photo and directing the searchlight gaze on me.

A good marriage?

Nothing can happen to us, Booth was saying, sitting on the edge of the bed in his undershorts, not ever. We were staying at a run-down hotel near Union Station, having left Ted parked with my father while we looked in Washington for a place to live briefly. I think, Booth said, looking down his nose and sitting up very straight and serious as he did when saying something immodest, that I will make quite a good deal of money. And, of course, however it turns out, I will love you till the day I die.

"It was a good marriage," I told Evan.

He looked bleakly at the horseshoe crab again, the ready victim waiting for the needle. He put the picture down on the desk, shoved his chair back impatiently and stood up.

"I don't know anything about this kind of thing," he said to the wall, "but since I met you everything is different. I can't sort it out." He stared at the wastebasket briefly and gave it an angry push with his foot, which caused it to roll on its side. "It's late in the game for this kind of thing to happen to me."

He crossed the room and put his arms around me.

"Does any of this matter to you?" he asked.

The late winter sunshine filtered through the blind and made an odd, round pattern on the floor. Outside an ambulance siren screamed, mingling with the sound of screeching brakes. I thought with some part of my mind that some poor devil was in trouble and with another part that you should watch out what you wish for because sometimes you get it.

"Yes," I said after a while, "but maybe not the way you want it to."

Here it was, everything I wanted, not crumbs but a heaping armload. It was balm, it was comfort, it was refuge. This nice, nice man had just indicated that I mattered to him. He was suggesting that we take a weekend together and sort things out. He was even looking at me.

"I don't know," I said, and I really didn't. "It seems so unreal, somehow. I'm practically sixty." It was the very first time I had said that out loud, let alone thought it. "I thought these were the golden years when everything diminuendoed, and now it is all kind of coming apart like a jigsaw puzzle."

He ignored all that.

"Will you go?" he asked, holding very tightly to my hand.

"It's awfully nice the way it is," I said. "I like it this way."

"What's the matter with me?" he demanded, and he was actually smiling. "Why does everyone get the idea that only the young are entitled to these things? Give us a chance, Elizabeth."

"No," I was saying into the phone, "I'm so sorry but I'm going out of town. Please think of me again, though. I would have loved to come."

I hung up, shaken. The Rubicon had just been crossed and I, the crosser, was the most surprised of all. I had had no idea what I was going to say until I said it. When I had picked up the phone, the weekend had still hung in the balance, a decision I was mulling over. Standing there barefoot in my bedroom among the balls and old shoes that Katie lugs upstairs with us every night, I had a sense of sitting in the audience, curtain going up, noting that the lady had made up her mind.

I stared at the dirty place on the wall where Joan had leaned for so many years while conducting the interminable telephone conversations of youth. In this room I had progressed from a young wife, to a suburban matron whose world centered on the success of her children, to a survivor in a suddenly alien world. And now the erstwhile matron, former cub-scout mother, chairman of the traffic committee and member of the country-club women's golf association, was about to join the ranks of those to whom a sexual encounter was an accepted part of life. Nothing in the world argued against it. Nobody could possibly care. Louis, had he known, would have been proud and delighted.

How lovely to to once again be possibly first with someone, not just a friend for odd moments, an obligation to be remembered, a fill-in for extra moments. To be needed and counted on, thought about. What could be wrong with something so right?

I became suddenly aware that two brown dog eyes

were boring holes in me. There was a delay in the usual routine that preceded dog walking. All right, all right, I said, and padded across the floor to the chest of drawers to get out a sweater. It was the same chest of drawers that had stood in my bedroom at home a thousand years ago, when I was a young girl. On the top left-hand corner was an ugly cigarette burn, which I personally had etched there when I forgot and left my sophisticated fag burning there behind me when I went downstairs to the party below.

I ran my finger over the blackened groove ruefully and stooped to the sweaters and, as I did, the tape did a fast back run and I was standing there before the same drawer, a girl in my early twenties, shaking out a brand new diaphanous black lace nightgown that had suddenly joined my flannel-footed pajamas.

"What do you think?" I was saying, dangling it before the wide eyes of my friend, Alice.

She was staring at it, stunned.

"But what in the world did you buy that for?" she demanded, lifting the folds that fell from the skirt with a tentative finger. "In this zero weather? Do you think you're Rita Hayworth?"

Years later, when I was an old married lady of more than a decade, she told me that she had known then that I was planning an affair with Booth. But I hadn't known. I was still thinking it over.

Across the years I sighed and selected a sweater from the pile. At the closet door I was so long choosing which pair of slacks that a cold nose nudged my leg. I reached blindly for a pair in the back of the closet and stooped to take the shoe trees from my walking shoes, making Katie at last happy.

The girl who bought that black nightgown so many years ago would have laughed at shoe trees.

* * *

"You seem terribly distracted lately," said Harriet over the edge of her teacup, blue eyes bright as a parakeet's, examining me. "Also jumpy. Is there something I should know? Is it that aficionado of the belly dance and butterflies?"

One of the things I plan to learn in my next life is to keep some secrets of my own. It seemed like a good place to start.

"I'm worried about money," I said. I was, too. Always and eternally. "I'm playing the lottery."

She sat up very straight. If there is one thing Harriet understands, it is worry about money. She knows everything about the beta factor and how to pay Uncle Sam as little as possible and how to get the most short-term interest with the least risk. The idea that she might be missing a bet on the lottery to get really rich excited her.

"Is there a system?" she demanded, all bright-eyed.

It was to laugh. If she had only seen me questioning the pensioners, the elderly who lined up at the machine in the drugstore with their hunch numbers, the first three digits of their social security number, their mother's birthday, the telephone-number exchange of their old boss. We had become instant friends, all of us, and I had so far ventured three dollars, all of which had vanished. I had tried, separately, the box, the combination and the straight. I had stood in line together with the construction workers and sharpies, exchanging hints and absorbing information from the pros. It was only as I was standing in line for the third time that it hit me like a revelation that the occasional dollar Booth had thrust into my hand to put on the lottery had not been a form of recreation, a silly whim, but a last desperate hope. He had known what lay ahead.

"No system," I told Harriet. Just a sort of shamed prayer.

"If you would like me to explain a little more about how to do it," said the ancient gentleman in front of me in line, struggling to manage the money in spite of a stroke-damaged arm, "I could give you my telephone number."

"Thank you," I said politely and took it all down.

"They say you have to keep at it to win," I told Harriet. "I wouldn't know."

She sank back into the cushions, looking crestfallen.

"Well, she said, "money isn't everything."

"Not if you've got it."

"What about love?"

"Please pass some my way."

We were silent, sipping the tea.

"What would you do," I said finally, "if you didn't have any money to invest and had to earn your keep?" The idea of Harriet in my shoes was hard to summon up.

She thought prettily, brow furrowed, stirring her tea with the spoon.

"I'd be a companion," she said at last, "to some difficult elderly lady. I'd manage her establishment with great charm and efficiency, and I wouldn't cheat her and I'd be very nice to her. She would come to depend on me. Then she would pass on and probably remember me in her will. In which case," she added, eyes sparkling, "I would take a flyer in second-tier stocks and increase it fivefold."

"You'd be very good at it," I said, and I meant it. But she didn't hear me. I had opened up a train of thought to which she was unaccustomed, a Pandora's box revealing disquieting things.

"Have you ever considered," she said slowly, cup halfway to her lips, "who will take care of us when we're old? Will the kids clap us into some nasty rest home where they don't change the sheets and the nurses are cross and we shuffle off to a terrible dinner at 5:30? And give us some hypodermics if we protest."

I looked at her fondly.

"If this should happen," I said, "you will be the belle of all two of the male inmates."

She was not to be beguiled. She gave a little shiver, put the teacup down and hugged her arms as if she felt a draft. Harriet, even briefly sobered, made me want to look away.

"What is it really like to wake up in an empty house?" she said. "There's so much noise and quarreling here that I think I long for silence, but I know if there weren't anyone here to order around and disagree with or leave dirty socks in the bathroom, I'd be desolate. You and Alexia seem so stalwart."

"What the hell, you do what is required," I said crossly. "Everybody does. You get used to a key at the neighbor's in case something happens."

But you never get used to having no one to tell things to.

"I wish I knew a charming, single, rich man to introduce you to, who would fall madly in love with you. One who would buy you diamonds and take you to expensive restaurants and of course be very good in bed. And you would bring him over here for dinner and I would flirt, but he would have eyes only for you."

"There aren't any like that," I said, "and don't worry about it. It is possible I have found a sort of—viable substitute."

Chapter 27

WE WERE standing, Evan and I, beside the Fiat in front of the inn I had chosen. It was none of those where we had lunched so many times, nothing familiar. I had wanted something removed from old associations, something for fresh starts. Only once before had I seen this ancient inn in Middleburg, Virginia, and that had been before my marriage.

"It's nice," said Evan, looking around him.

I looked at him while he looked at Middleburg. He seemed out of place somehow, too intense and inward to fit in this retreat for people who have their money. Because of this I loved him especially. I have always preferred people who don't quite fit, who are alien in the crowd.

It was a long way from the stalled traffic knots of New

York, and he stood for a moment taking it all in before bending to the Fiat to extract our bags. Even the Fiat seemed a stranger among the station wagons and the self-consciously utilitarian cars from the surrounding estates. The Fiat looked as if it were expected at work Monday morning.

At the registration desk I hung back while Evan dealt with the clerk. I wondered idly if he were registering as Mr. and Mrs., but it didn't matter. Once it had mattered a great deal, when I was twenty-three and hanging back nervously at the Ritz in Boston, twisting my dead mother's wedding ring nervously and wondering if the clerk would know at once that Booth and I were not married to each other but contemplating illicit love. But this was the last thing I wanted to think about now.

The young girl at the desk had no interest in our affairs. She led the way up the old broad stairway to our room on the second floor, gave us the key and disappeared. Evan put the bags on the floor and stood staring out at the village street below, running a hand through his thinning hair. From his back it was impossible to know what he was thinking.

I was staring at the enormous double bed between the windows.

"I'm not very good in a double bed," I said after a while, not looking at him.

He turned then and stared at me wordlessly.

"I didn't mean that the way it sounds," I said. "It's just that I discovered a long time ago that I can't keep still long enough to sleep in double beds."

A long time ago. I was seeing my father's German cook, hugging the mixing bowl and stirring the batter, listening to the news that I was engaged.

"Marriage ain't all beer and skittles," she said, and her

words were full of satisfaction, clueing me in with all the venom of the bad fairy at the christening. And in the double bed on the night of our wedding, when the champagne had worn off, I thought of her. It had nothing to do with sex or love or the partner I had chosen for life, but I needed space of my own. I need, have always needed, needed even then room to thrash about, blankets all my own to wrap about me as I choose. Happy to share my love but not a bed, I clung with my fingers to the edge of my territory and thought of Cook. This is what she meant, I thought bleakly. Marriage means a double bed all my life.

I was wrong.

"That," said Booth the next morning as we arose, "was the worst night I ever spent in all my life." And he stepped to the phone to order a room with twin beds.

"Don't you like double beds?" said Evan. "I'll speak to the girl when we go down."

The dining room was dark and cavernous, wandering off into all sorts of alcoves and nooks so that it was at once large and intimate. Unhurried patrons in expensive tweeds sat eating and drinking by the soft light from the mullioned windows. The waitress smiled, led us to a table in the corner and departed.

It was a pleasant room, and I didn't mind that Evan seemed to have lapsed into one of his silences. They no longer disturbed me. Silences move from uneasy to comfortable when you get to know people. I let my mind drift, feeling good about the inn, good about Evan. I opened the menu, debating what to choose.

It is odd how you notice the small details of things around you when important things happen to you. The doctor comes out of the operating room to tell you whether or not the tumor was malignant, and what your mind registers is that he seems to have a mole just under his left eye. He speaks and you hear, you even absorb what he is saying, but your attention is centered on the mole.

In this way I remember the left-over cigarette bent in the ashtray on our table. The whole scene is etched forever on my mind, like a stage set prepared beforehand onto which we two had wandered by some design beyond us, trailing unresolved doubts and tentative tendrils of hope, while the world ground inexorably on as if nothing of importance were happening. I remember how the light struck the single spray of mums in the vase on the table, and the exact pattern of the type of the menu, because I was studying it at the time.

"I think," said Evan, not even looking at me, appearing to study his own huge menu, "that maybe I love you."

I sat very still while the carillon boomed all around me, listening to the reverberations of his words. He took off his glasses, and then apparently thinking better of it, put them back and studied me over the top of them. The impact of the gray eyes made me turn away.

"Do you mind?" he asked quite simply, and I managed to shake my head. I was busy picking up the pieces of my reason.

The waitress bustled up, dressed like a Colonial farm wife, and looked expectantly at Evan, pencil poised.

"Drink?" she asked brightly.

He looked at the wine list briefly and ordered a bottle of Pouilly Fuissé. She nodded and disappeared.

"Was that all right?" he wanted to know.

"No," I said. "I saw the price. It was absurd."

He smiled, and I thought that he looked as nearly happy as I had ever seen him.

"You have to do something recklessly foolish every once in a while," he said. "Perpetual thrift shrivels the soul. Once in a while you have to buy the very best, whether or not you have the money. Something terribly extravagant and outrageously unnecessary. If you don't like the wine, we'll send it back. Or we'll throw it on the floor. This is a day for foolish gestures."

The wine arrived, and he solemnly tasted it and waved an acquiescence. And we were alone again.

He was behaving as if it were the most natural thing in the world that he should say what he had said and that I should be the one he said it to. And, suddenly, this man so fond of silences was doing all the talking.

"I always thought life was a sort of shipwreck," he said, peering at me over the rim of his wineglass. "My marriage was disastrous, and I kept looking everywhere for something else. I went from bad to worse and then I quit. Quit hoping and trying. And now, just as I had gotten used to not expecting anything, here you come into my life. And for the first time since I can remember, I'm happy again."

I looked at him across the table, hunched over his expensive wine, hair falling a little into one eye, and I wanted to put my arms around him. This taciturn, melancholy man had carefully unwrapped something inside and handed it across the table to me as a gift. And no matter what he had in mind, I needn't be lonely anymore, could know that wherever I went, whatever I was doing, there was somebody who cared about my return.

Somewhere back a way, when everybody I know was trying to pay school tuition and survive rock and the new math, Frank Sinatra assured us over three million radios that love's more comfortable the second time around. I couldn't remember what else he said about it, and briefly I wished I could. Love in your twenties comes so naturally. You play it by ear, read it off the stars, doubts don't exist, no questions arrive. You fall into bed, you love, it is so uncomplicated. Now I could have done with some guidelines.

"Eat your hamburg," Evan was saying solicitously. "I didn't mean to scare away your appetite. Hamburger goes so well with Pouilly Fuissé."

I picked up my fork again and pushed some food into another place on my plate. I could feel his eye on me.

"Is what I said so—well, hell, unwelcome?" he said.

The choice of adjective made me smile, in the course of which I discovered I was fighting a lump in my throat. Louis was right. I was a Brontë heroine. The wine and the way he was looking at me made me feel lightheaded. I fumbled in my bag for a handkerchief and blew my nose. Everything I could possibly want was being dumped into my lap, and I was behaving like a schoolgirl. A schoolgirl, hell, a fool.

I pushed the food around some more, and Evan reached for his wallet.

"This is absurd," he said. "Let's take a walk and you show me the village. You're obviously not going to eat that, and I want to avoid the moment when you say, 'This is so sudden.'"

We threaded our way through the people killing the hours over coffee and out into a perfect early-March day, pale watery sunshine patterning the old sidewalks like the promise of spring to follow. He reached for my hand and we walked up the side street not saying anything at all. The March wind was blowing my hair, but I didn't care. I knew that only young girls look well with the wind in their hair, but none of this mattered. I had blundered into never-never land and all the rules were suspended.

We passed an old man who had dragged his chair from the store to tilt his face up into the late winter sunshine. We passed a woman in a tweed coat looking very hurried and a child wearing jodhpurs and a little velvet riding hat. I looked up at Evan and smiled at him and thought how happy I was. The only trouble was I wasn't really.

I didn't know this at first. It was a gift, this possible love of his, making the world safe and warm again, reassuring me, slaying with one blow all the beasts lurking in the shadows. I am loved, therefore I am. But with every step we took, I longed to go back to where we had been. I wanted everything to stop right here and on this day, at this moment. Because there was deep water out there, and I wasn't ready. I wanted to wade around in it close to shore.

We stopped in front of a window on a little side street, a window banked by boxwood and old brick, packed with hand-painted china ornamented with foxes, riding boots, crops, cocktail glasses with horses' heads. I stared at them for a while, studying the toys of the rich as if I were on an anthropological expedition, and thought with some part of my mind that somebody should start a society for the protection of foxes outnumbered fifteen to one by dogs and horses and riders out for amusement.

And the more I stared into the window, the more I felt uneasy.

Evan looked at me and then came around and got between me and the fox-painted china.

"I don't like the way you look," he said.

"It's the way I look," I said. "You'll have to get used to it."

He was not put off.

"Something's got off the track," he said, not making it a question, holding me by the shoulders in both hands, looming over me and blotting out riding boots.

Looking up at him, I felt a little sick. I thought that he was probably the most sensitive, the decentest, the nicest man I was ever again likely to meet and that there was no reason in the world why I couldn't truly love him for the rest of my life. All the time I was thinking this, I was trying not to cry. I loosened his hands and leaned my forehead against the cold glass of the store window, causing the pretty girl inside to look up in alarm.

"I don't know what's wrong with me," I said.

In the distance a dog was barking, and high up above us in the apartment over the store I thought I heard people laughing.

He caught my shoulder and turned me to face him.

"Tell me what's wrong," he said, and his face was etched with lines I never saw before. He studied my face as if he were reading it, translating an ancient and difficult language, and then suddenly he let me go so that I staggered slightly to keep from falling. When he spoke he had turned away so I could scarcely hear his words.

"I'm not the one, am I?" he said.

He was the one. How could he not be?

"I don't know," I said, furiously kicking the pile of leftover leaves next to the boxwood. "I don't know anything much anymore. Maybe I'm an emotional cripple. Maybe he took part of me with him that's essential. Of course I love you. Anybody who knows you would love you. I even love that dumb Fiat of yours because it reminds me of you. I love walking down the street with you and sitting across the table from you and picnicking on your office floor."

He didn't say anything at all.

"But I don't seem to want anything more than that," I said. "That's as far as I can go. I can't help it."

The pretty girl inside the shop was now openly staring at us through the window, a voyeur as I snipped my life into rags. I managed to look at Evan and saw what I knew I was going to see. His face had taken on its old careful expression, as if he had known all along that we weren't winners, that fourteen-karat happiness was for other people and that we would have to mush along with bits and pieces.

"Nothing stays the way it is," he said, and I knew he was right.

I put my arms around him and closed my eyes. I couldn't bear to look at Middleburg, or him, or the entire world, for that matter.

"Yell at me," I said. "Blame me. It would make me feel better."

"What do you want?" he whispered in my ear. "What do you want that I can't give you?"

When I opened my eyes, the girl inside the store was very busy rearranging a cigarette box with a fox's head beside a mohair tweed lap robe. I caught her eye, and she gave me the kind of look you give a drunk on the street, a carefully blank, removed look. I gave her a little wave so she wouldn't feel left out.

"I don't know what I want," I said. "That's the whole trouble."

"Maybe," he said, "maybe we should have met a long time ago. But then we would both have been different people and probably would have hated each other."

"It's nothing to do with you," I said, desperate to smooth out the pain in this whole terrible moment. "Nothing at all about you."

"Of course not," he said and laughed, but it was the wrong kind of laughter.

"It's me," I said, fighting the tears. "It's me that's the trouble. I think I'm missing a vital part." I groped shamelessly for his hand.

He put his arms around me then and dropped a kiss on the top of my head, a comforting kiss, empty of urgency and desire, the kind of kiss you give a child when you're saying good-bye.

"I suppose," he said, "that we ought, under the circumstances, to be thinking about going back to town tonight. I suppose that maybe, considering, the double bed is a mistake."

He looked down at me and I could ready nothing except that he wanted to know if I agreed.

When we left the pretty girl and her fox wares, Evan kept a little distance between us on the sidewalk.

All the long way home he was silent. He peered through the windshield intently, retracing the thruways we had taken so companionably together earlier in the day. I couldn't think of anything to say, couldn't shake the sense that I had cut some final cord, lost something very valuable. I wished fervently that I were dead.

The Fiat nosed at last to the curb of my house, and he went up the steps to the door with me. I was crying when he opened the screen door to let me slip my key into the lock.

"Are you going out of my life?" I asked, fumbling blindly with the key. Lots of girls know when to shut up, but I have always hated loose ends.

He looked at his feet and then shook his head, as if they had told him what to say.

"We'll see each other," he said. "How could we help it?"

When I heard the car recede into the distance, I lay down on the bed without bothering to undress. I knew that the sound of a Fiat would always give me a pang.

Chapter 28

ACTUALLY I did see Evan again, but I wished I hadn't. I took the work I had done for *Wilderness Ways* down to lay it on his desk, and he was there. The sight of him hunched over a layout, totally engrossed, thinking about the future of the American crocodile while his tie kept getting in the way, seemed to blot out everything that had happened since we last met in this office. But then he looked up, and I knew I was mistaken. His face was shuttered, careful about letting anything inside out.

"Hello," he said, and waited.

Looking at him now was worse than what had gone before. It was like the morning after the operation when you just begin to understand how you hurt. I shuffled my papers to keep everything as businesslike as possible and put them on his desk. I wished already that I had mailed in my article, let it all go as it was. There was no way to fix anything, salvage any pieces. But the thought of the job going out of my life with the man gave me a cold feeling in the stomach.

I asked about that.

He looked at me, and the expression was gentle.

"As long as I'm editor, you can have all the work you want," he said. "And when I move on, somebody else will want your work. Don't worry about that."

When I move on. Well, under the circumstances, what difference? Maybe it would be better. I wanted to ask him where he might be going but I didn't feel I knew him well enough anymore.

Anything would be better than standing there among the wreckage, and I squared up the papers again and moved toward the door.

"Evan?"

My hand was on the doorjamb, but I couldn't leave it like this. He was looking at me, and the way he looked hurt.

"Maybe it would be better if I mailed the next one in."

I thought at first he was going to protest, but then I saw that I was wrong.

"Maybe," he said finally, looking somewhere just above my head. "Maybe even probably."

And that was how it ended. I heard later he had taken a job in California, but by that time I had walled off the scar tissue.

Things were infinitely harder without him, full of what if's and backward glances. It was like having warmed myself by a fire that had suddenly gone out, and it seemed he had taken with him my last hope of a future that mattered. The sense of aloneness attacked me in unguarded moments, in the middle of the night, at parties while the talk swirled around me. It was all encapsulated when I braked the car and automatically, unable to lose the habit of years, put a hand to pull back the long-departed child beside me and got only a handful of Katie hair.

I tried not to dwell on it, but I felt a landslide of people departing my life in one way or another. On every side of me people seemed to live in a warm maelstrom of protective family and friends, while I alone was solo. Then, as if to prove my point, Frieda, once before snatched back from the edge of eternity, went into a serious decline.

At first I thought I could cope with the difficulty. I took to shutting her in the kitchen at night, confining her to a small, easily cleaned space. But every morning when I opened the door, spreading puddles greeted me, and when she ate her dinner, she ate it ravenously but lying down. Her back legs were no longer dependable and, though we still took our morning walk, we walked at a funereal pace which she accomplished mostly sidewise, like a crab.

I prayed for a fatal heart attack in the night, but she lived on, infirm and incontinent, scarcely aware of anything but the hour of mealtime. In my dreams she appeared young and bright-eyed, once more scrambled over the back fence with agile feet in the chain-link loops. Sometimes she sat beside Booth in the sun on the front steps, watching the world go by, alert and interested. Sometimes she dissolved into other dogs who had preceded her—Charlie, the white half-spritz; Clancy, my father's scotty who had waited only two days to join him in death; a succession of setters stretching back into my childhood.

And then one gray morning I opened my eyes and

knew that today was the day. This time there would be no reprieve.

I have loved a great many dogs in my life, most of which lived so long they had to be helped from this world, but never before have I had to pass sentence on my own, a jury of one, without consultation, without someone beside me to mourn. George, who came before Frieda, underwent an expensive ten days' course of vitamins and geriatric pills at the vet's before we gave up hope of keeping him alive any longer. Even then, it was Booth, not I, who made the telephone call ordering the hypodermic.

Now there was no hiding place. I got down her leash for the last time from its accustomed place by the door and got her to her feet. With Katie, dancing with excitement about us, we went down the steps to the driveway together, past the rhododendron, past the butterfly bush not doing well this year, past the place behind the house where she had lain in her prime when the day was too hot. She felt her way down cautiously, paw extended to feel the edge of the step, making the last descent. I opened the door of the car, and Katie hopped in. I picked Frieda up and stuffed her in beside Katie, and shut the door on them dry-eyed.

Twice she fell off the seat and scrabbled painfully back up. Once, halfway there, I thought I would turn around. It was touch and go and I slowed the car, but then I remembered how the woman we met on our morning walk had leaned over her solicitously, shaking her head.

"The poor old thing," she had murmured, "the poor, poor old thing."

We drove into the vet's driveway, and I reached for her leash. "Stay there," I said to Kate, stay in this world, Katie, and took Frieda's leash to make the slow trip across the parking lot to the door. The smells excited her, and she squatted to urinate, making her mark for the last time—I was here.

I opened the door and urged her through, and she lifted her old head to sniff the animal smell, pungent as the approach to a circus tent. We were behind a woman holding in her arms a toy poodle with a bow in its hair. The poodle was troubled with diarrhea. We waited, Frieda and I.

The poodle was all right for days at a time but then, for no good reason, he had a bad bout with his bowels. The woman explained this all earnestly, as the poodle fixed the receptionist with a bright, unwinking eye. It took quite a while to report the details, and so it was some time before the receptionist turned to me and asked if I wanted her to take Frieda.

I had called ahead, not wanting any wait in the death cell, and she held out her arms wordlessly.

Until this moment I had been in a sort of deep freeze, marveling at my own composure, watching Frieda bumbling about on her leash at my feet, knowing that by my decree, this was her last day on earth, but not really believing it. But when the actual moment came, I dropped my head into my hands and burst into noisy sobs.

"How much," I managed to stammer, "does it cost to kill a dog?"

The silence was total. I slipped the leash to my wrist and used the freed hand to help staunch the strange sounds issuing from my mouth. In the process, I dropped my sunglasses, and the poodle's mother, at last recognizing priorities, bent to pick them up. The receptionist, looking frightened, said hurriedly that they would send a bill.

No bill to relive again this terrible moment.

"I want to pay now," I cried like a petulant child. I scrabbled in my purse and extracted a twenty-dollar bill.

"It's ten," said the receptionist, seeing that there was no escape from this insistent woman. She came around the side of the desk and held out her arms to receive Frieda. She didn't look at me. She was very busy unbuckling the blue collar with the pseudojewels that Frieda had worn so many years, trotting up the street on business of her own when we were all young and the world belonged to us.

I leaned down and laid my cheek against her old head, put my arms around her. Nobody stirred, the poodle's diarrhea and my twenty-dollar bill forgotten. And then they were whisking her out of my sight. Somebody put a folded bill in my hand, and the poodle's mother opened the door for me. I stumbled through, wordless now and beyond tears, to a world diminished once again. When I opened the door of the car and got in, Katie, sensing trouble, nosed her way under my arm so she could lean close.

Frieda was gone. It was over, but the world must go on, so I drove into the first gas station for gas. As I attended to the nozzle, watching the little numbers chasing themselves in the pump window and thinking what a canine reception committee awaited me in heaven, Katie pressed her nose to the glass and wagged her tail, keeping an eye on me.

The snaggle-toothed attendant showed up to collect the money and looked expressionless into the backseat where Kate sat, erect and friendly, hoping to make his acquaintance.

He counted out my change slowly as if the transaction were difficult, taking his time, his gnarled old hands clumsy with the bills. I was stuffing the money in my wallet, ready to drive away, when I noticed he was still standing by the window.

"Don't you have a husband?" he growled.

Don't I have a husband? Why did he want to know? Because I was jockeying my own gas? His front teeth were filed or had worn away to a point, to several points, and he looked strangely like a bat or a small rodent. I drew back.

"Why do you ask?" I said.

"If you had a husband," he said, "you wouldn't have to love a dog like that."

And he turned away.

I called the children to tell them the news. They were curiously contained, whether from lack of concern or from self-restraint, it was impossible to tell. Perhaps to them she had already gone, perhaps they thought that, old, she could not take much pleasure in life anyway. They were kind, solicitous, regretful, removed. The young do not understand that being old does not necessarily mean you are ready to die.

Now the small bokhara in the hall was empty of everything but a few hairs she had left behind. They would be swept up on Thursday when Mary came. Mary, who knew Frieda as a puppy, always endured Katie's lavish welcome and politely excused herself to pat Frieda's grizzled old head. Mary would grieve.

And I. Because that old blind deaf dog needed me, and everybody needs to be needed.

Chapter 29

"WHAT WILL it be like?" I asked wistfully, sitting in Alexia's living room having a farewell cocktail. Alexia was moving away to be nearer her daughter, abandoning the new little house into which she had moved like a hermit crab changing shells after George's death. Abandoning her house, abandoning me. She didn't seem to mind either one. Her eyes were preoccupied, fixed on yet another house.

"It's small," she said. "All on one floor."

I could see she had already, in her mind, departed, her center removed to this unknown house in a city I didn't know. It was now simply a matter of tedious lingering details to be wound up. She was going back to her people, to the city where she had been a young girl.

"I wish there were a picture," I said morosely.

I like to visualize the people I am fond of in the places where they live their lives. I wanted to be able to imagine the kitchen in which she would drink a midmorning cup of coffee, the garden in which she would grow things unknown to me that thrive in mountain climates. Otherwise she would seem to vanish like a puff of smoke, a half-forgotten face attached to a telephone number now belonging to somebody else.

"The climate is much better," she was saying, self-contained, unworried, a woman with all problems solved. "I have always hated the heat."

I wanted her to say she felt a pang at what she was leaving behind, but I knew she wouldn't. Alexia's life is a song in which you can hear only the high notes, while the bass, thumping away with the beat of things that can't be changed, is ignored. I always want to say it out loud, point out that things are being swept under the rug, but then that doesn't really do any good, and perhaps she is right.

"It isn't as if I'm leaving the house George and I lived in," she said, serene and detached. "I've already weeded out the nonessentials."

But what is a nonessential? Would she think the sheaf of letters from the first grade thanking me for being room mother, all painstakingly compressed between large blue lines, spelled out with stubby pencils, was a nonessential? The perfect swallowtail butterfly I plucked from the radiator grill of the car, dead but miraculously preserved and now adorning my kitchen shelf? Weed these out and you have a nice neat and perfectly ordered house. Sterile as an autumn leaf.

"Yes, I know," I said. "I'm sure you'll be very happy out there."

I sounded polite. I didn't know this Alexia. She

seemed to have passed beyond my reach, and it made me feel sad. Perhaps I was also a nonessential.

You're going to leave a hole in my life, I wanted to cry, but it would have embarrassed her. And what is the answer to that, anyway? And it was, of course, only the beginning. Harriet, younger than I by far, was already planning where she and her husband would go when his retirement came through. Ceci, with whom I play golf, was even now building a house for the sunset years in a golfing resort. Two can go anywhere, and sometimes one, if she's only going home. But there was nowhere I wanted to go. New York is my city, though I didn't envision having to live in it alone without my friends.

And then there was this other cloud on the horizon. I was going to be sixty.

Is sixty so terrible? Everything is gradual—one day you're fifty-nine and the next sixty, and it's after all only one more day. You don't get old overnight. It's something you've known about all along.

None of this is true. Sixty, alone, looms like a frightening hurdle. At sixty you stand at a plateau below which stretch dreadful things to contemplate, and you know that, like it or not, you're going to get a close look. The valley below is mined with perils like retirements, diseases of the elderly, age spots, kind relatives who make allowances for you, a yellow brick road which turns a corner around which you cannot see and would probably rather not. Thirty is nothing compared to sixty, though you don't know it at the time, believing that sixty is for other people. Forty is rather nice, the prime time with the sun out and the kids out of diapers and everything looking possible. Fifty I don't remember much. I didn't take much notice.

Life at the turn of the decade appeared to be an address

book with a great many names crossed out, with no safe place anywhere, like the beltway at rush hour in the rain. How had Robert coped in that grand apartment, all alone with his infirmities? How was Louis able to thumb his nose at the statistics, to remain elegantly slim, interested and even in demand? For that matter, how did Booth manage? Into my mind's eye came his image standing in a phone booth outside some factory in January, two months before his death, the hand holding the receiver shaking with the effect of radiation but talking earnestly into the phone. From the warmth of the car, I watched him talking to the invisible man who had not shown up at the interview, and I saw that his face was gray with fatigue and pain.

He was sixty-four at the time. What then is sixty?

I put it out of my mind. Too much thought given to this kind of thing, I told myself, and as if it had been waiting for that moment, the phone rang and the voice on the other end of the line was Joan's. She was coming home, she said. It hadn't worked out in Georgia. Would it be all right if she lived with me for a little while till she got another job?

It would be all right, I said into the phone, and she rang off, having changed the entire color of the world.

Twelve hours later I saw her emerging from her little second-hand Toyota, stuffed to the ceiling and the jumbled overflow lashed to the roof. I could distinguish a folding lawn chair and a broom and what appeared to be a music stand. The rest was a blur.

Over and over we are told not to count on our children. They have their lives to live; we ours; they are lent to us; let them go when they're ready. All I know is that she brought the sunshine with her. And a mountain of dirty laundry, a couple of installment credit books on the car and her last year at college, and a strong breath of optimism, which had been in scarce supply.

For twenty-four hours she staggered in and out of the house, carrying the floating pieces of her life with which the Toyota was stuffed, the messy odds and ends of possessions that the young collect. I watched without really believing it possible that it all came from one car. Armloads of records, old shoes, usually with one missing, bottles of half-used shampoo, a cane someone had made for her as a present, a wardrobe of floppy hats and a thousand boxes of paperbacks, mostly soaked with soy sauce from a bottle that had leaked. It was like watching the Austin in ring three of the circus disgorge eighteen midgets from its miniature interior.

Once again the house was full to bursting, and the lights burned extravagantly late into the night. Katie, who had been my faithful shadow, now flirted her tail and galloped up the stairs in quest of a piece of bare floor in Joan's bedroom on which to lie and worship. When the idol was out, she lay in the bedroom door, ever on the watch for her return. I didn't mind but I pretended I did.

It wasn't easy to find a job.

"Where are you going?" I would ask as she paused in the doorway, an Oliver Twist cap pulled down over one eye, long cardigan flapping, counterculture newspaper under one arm.

"There's an ad for an editorial aide," she would murmur vaguely and close the door behind her, leaving Katie to peer mournfully after her through the curtains, muddy paws braced against the mail slot.

She left the water running. One night she left the back door open wide all night. Shoes proliferated in the hall, and the full orange juice pitcher was emptied overnight.

She put dishes where I do not put them and she used the house as a bed and breakfast, a sort of pit stop in which to shower and sleep. She did not take out the trash. She mowed half the lawn, but her friends, who hadn't been instructed, called at ten thirty when I was asleep. Her room looked like a school white elephant sale. No matter. I wasn't alone anymore.

This is not to say that I didn't fret. When she called me at two in the morning to say she was sleeping over with Lucy, I couldn't get back to sleep. I felt the difference in the relationship. She was not my daughter; she was a young woman I had taken in when she needed a place. She was dependent, but then so was I. I loved having her there.

"You're going to have a birthday," she said quite matter-of-factly over the dish of grits laced with sorghum syrup with vitamin A added. It didn't sound like a catastrophe when she said it. "We have to celebrate."

Celebrate? Well, why not? There she was, out of a job, in hock to the bank, not even in love at twenty-four, and she sang in the shower. It was an inspirational message courtesy of my own genes. Everything will be all right if you only think it will.

"I'm sixty," I began tentatively. "That's old country. Best not to call attention to it." She went on steadily spooning up the grits, not paying attention. "What kind of a party do you think we should have?"

It was a very nice party. Different, but then being sixty is not like other birthdays, either. Joan asked a lot of very low-key young men and a handful of pretty, self-contained young women who were very friendly, and I added a few of my own friends. She made a huge batch of something that was largely eggplant and roots and berries, which everybody said was delicious, and we all sat on the floor and drank wine from a gallon jug and discussed life. Scott Joplin played his rags on the stereo, and even though somebody kicked over the wine jug on the rug, we got the stain up immediately. And just for the moment getting older didn't matter much anymore, and I felt there would always be somebody there if I only knew where to look.

When they had all gone and we were washing up the mess—or rather when I was washing up and Joan was having a cup of tea—she told me she had fallen in love briefly with somebody in Georgia and that hadn't worked out any better than the job. She dropped a tear into her teacup as she told me, a small tear for a brief encounter, and I looked at her with something that was a strange combination of love and envy. How splendid to mark the passing of a love affair with proper regret and yet to know, as she surely did, that around the corner is bound to be the one to make you forget, to dim the pain of the one that failed with the shiny radiance of the real thing.

After a while I said so.

"I guess so," she said, stirring the tea, which is always awash with milk since France. "But there's no guarantee."

"There's no guarantee for anything," I told her, and I felt like the bad fairy at the christening. Why go around telling people that there's a joker in every pack and that all bets are hedged and all you can do is stumble on hopefully, crossing your fingers? "But if you want to know the truth," I told her, "I still believe in everything, except the tooth fairy. I'm just a little more cautious."

She thought about it for a while, and then she looked

at me in a way that I know precedes something she was worried about having to say.

"It's not that I don't want to live with you," she began, "but you know I'll be moving out when I get a job and enough money. You know that, don't you? I feel it's kind of a step backward, coming home like a little girl. It's nothing to do with you. It's just that I need to be independent."

I shut the dishwasher and went to put my arms around her.

"Nobody could understand that better than me."

"Better than I," she said looking relieved.

It's time for children to move on when they correct your grammar.

"Good-bye," Alexia was saying, "we'll keep in touch, won't we?"

Another good-bye, no better because I knew it was coming. I keep rearranging them all in my subconscious, denying them when the lights are out. When I dream these days it is often of my father's house, before I had to sell it and somebody amputated its front porch and put aluminum siding on it. In the dream my father is not yet dead and Booth is somebody I have not yet met. Familiar things surround me in my father's house. I know exactly what is in the drawer of the hall table and which part of the pattern in the Oriental rug the sun will be picking out when I go out to pick up the *Rome Sentinel* from the porch. I know what to expect here. When I look in the mirror later, to comb my hair before I go to the dance, the only good-bye I can imagine is a matter of a separation over a vacation.

"Of course," I told Alexia. "You are looking at your

new pen pal. The mailman says I may prevent a rise in first-class postage rates all by myself."

"Will you come out ever, do you think?"

I shook my head. Let's not fool ourselves.

"You can't be sure," she said, and got up to get another cigarette. She bent over the box, and I noticed that she had gotten much thinner, very svelte really, but it was not the figure of a girl. "You might fall in love with an attractive man with money who will take you anywhere you want to go. And then you'll come."

"Who knows?" I said.

Who can be sure of anything? Things interfere that you didn't count on—the doctor's verdict, making a living, the changing face of love.

Conversation lagged as we faced each other across the room. We had already parted but nobody wanted to remark on it, and we spoke of her daughter and taxes in her new city compared to taxes in mine. I was thinking that inevitably thirty-five years of friendship would dwindle to the package at Christmas, the telephone call at birthdays, and that both of us knew it.

"I'm glad you have Joan back in town," she said, and after a while she got in her car and drove away out of my life. I thought of something later I wanted to tell her, but when I called, the number had already been disconnected.

"Work," Louis was saying over the elegant little French lamb chops, "is the panacea for everything. Plus, of course, a healthy relationship or two including sex."

We were sitting in one of his favorite restaurants in midtown Manhattan, watching the maitre d' carve a Peking duck with the skill of a surgeon.

He peered at me curiously across the table, and I thought that I really loved this enormously obsessed man.

"Is there anyone in your life?" he inquired. "A nice girl like you should have worked something out by now."

"Nothing," I said, shaking my head. Louis always makes it sound as if sex were a vitamin you added to your breakfast cereal if you were sufficiently enlightened. Wild horses on bended knee would not have dragged from me any mention of Evan. "But sometimes I think I must secretly long to lay it all on some capable man."

He was all attention.

"I have this recurrent fantasy," I said, "in which a faceless stranger walks into the middle of my life and takes over. The water heater in the basement is broken or I have lighted a fire with the damper still closed and smoke is pouring into the room and I am frantically looking for the right telephone number to get help. And as I am running my finger down the list of numbers in the Yellow Pages, this man emerges from the kitchen and he takes the phone from my hand.

"'Let me,' he says, and I surrender it to him, slipping back into the child-wife role. I point to the deluge in the cellar or the smoke billowing to the living room ceiling and step back respectfully.

"Is it Booth?" asked Louis, leaning forward with interest. "This man is Booth?"

"No, no, no," I told him impatiently. "Mechanics were not his strong point."

"Do you ever visualize what might happen when the water stops pouring out of the heater and the smoke is cleared away?"

"We never get that far."

He looked disappointed.

"But what kind of a fantasy life is that?" I demanded crossly, pushing the grains of rice on my plate into a neat group at one side. "Three years of running my own life and I'm thinking up some man to cope with crises. It's not rational. As a matter of fact I would have a hard time these days laying my head on anyone else's shoulder. I'm not looking to merge my identity again."

He spread his hands and smiled.

"See your psychiatrist."

How like Louis to assume I had one.

It was a very short time really until Joan found a job. Not the job she would hope for, but one in which she could be relatively happy and solvent. She was absorbed once more into a circle of friends which had missed her, and a few weeks later I overheard her tell Lucy in one of the telephone conversations that she was looking for a room in town.

I waited until she was ready to tell me, until she had found a place. There was no hurry, really. But in the meantime, nights when I woke the sense of aloneness returned multiplied like a family of rabbits. I lay on my back in the dark and wished I had been born in an age when families stayed together or nearby, and roots were familial rather than generational. Then I would pound the pillow angrily and explain to myself that no one ever should rely on a daughter to fill any gap. Nothing could be more unsuitable. It was only that it had been nice to have her around.

Through the window I watched my neighbor, a widow two years younger than I, coming and going, busy with her grandchildren, her church, her bridge parties. I didn't fit there, either. I alone was destined to make do with pleasantries from the acned clerk at Safeway, spend my evenings with my dog. Out there somewhere there must be somebody for me to talk to. I made resolutions to join the Foreign Movie Club, the Society for Odd Persons Without Connections. But I knew I was too busy scratching for a living.

"I'll be in the same city this time," said Joan, pushing her hair back and looking worried. Joan understands when she is leaving a hole. "I really have to do it, if only because of the bus schedule."

"Go," I said, very busy washing off the strawberries at the sink. "I'll get back my dog's affections. And some room in the hall closet."

So a week later we loaded up the little car again with old shoes and hats and tennis rackets and odd pots and pans and headed toward the city. The Toyota went first, riding low to the ground, and I came along behind in the Ford, a convoy for a new beginning, a mother whale escorting her baby into the open sea.

We drew to a halt in front of the crumbling elegance of her new address, and housemates emerged to help carry in things, the flotsam and jetsam of the caravan. They were scruffy and deferential to me and very friendly, and I loved them all at once.

"You'll be all right, won't you?" she said, leaning over an armload of John Coltrane records, brushing away some of the hair with an edge of the pile. She was already distracted, involved, part of this new life.

"Certainly," I told her, though I had scarcely ever felt less all right. But after all, this wasn't a real parting. "Come out soon or Katie will waste away." And I waved good-bye to the others and turned the little white Ford once more toward home, with Katie staring sadly back through the rear window.

The light is long at the crosstown intersection that takes me home, and I had time to think. I was remembering the house we were going home to when it was full of people coming home and sitting down for dinner and telling each other what happened to them all day. And I thought about what had happened since then, leaving me beached like a shipwreck on the sand, and what I had learned along the way. And in spite of the part of me I had just left behind, I knew that it was true that I would be all right. Maybe not happy, but all right.

For a while it would be harder to get the hang of being alone again. The bedrooms would be emptier and the house quieter after the lights were turned on. But once you've made your peace with being by yourself, learned to depend on you when that's all you've got, it doesn't seem so fearsome. The light changed, and I turned up the avenue and, tooling along in the late-afternoon grayish sunshine, I realized that I had crossed some sort of Rubicon from which there was no turning back and that I had somehow made myself into a person who could survive, and that there was satisfaction in that. The things that happen to you that hurt create antibodies that protect you like a vaccine. If life doesn't change you, it's not worth living.

Katie gave up her vigil and came and did her flypaper act, glueing herself against me and putting her nose on my shoulder, to the peril of traffic on the avenue. She leaned against me, giving me a thoughtful kiss, and I wondered if in time, I might not also learn to sing in the shower.

And what more could I possibly want?

I want it all not to have happened.

* * *

So all right, I am alone, but not really alone. Because there are ten and a half million of me out there—Alexia in her new little house, and Alo, who stood beside me the day I was married, and Emily, my neighbor, and Helen, with whom I have been playing golf all these years. And all the women left behind every day, whose names are listed among the survivors in the obituary columns.

Once I called up Alo, who is six months my senior in widowhood and therefore possibly aware of some secret not yet vouchsafed to me, and told her that I was discouraged, down and scared.

There was a pause, and I waited anxiously to hear what she had learned, what comforting words she would choose. I knew there weren't any answers to my problem, but irrationally I believed that she would find them. I could see her in my mind, considering her advice, pushing her hair back behind her ear with that gesture so familiar to me since we first met as college freshmen.

Her reply was soft, and the Boston accent slurred its edges.

"Hello, sister," she said.

Most of us, unless we are the exception, outlive the men we marry. It is a probability built into every marriage vow, the specter at the wedding feast and something of which we choose not to think. We tend to marry men older than we, and then of course women are simply tougher. The years alone are slated before we begin.

But oddly, there are compensations. You cannot imagine that this can be true in the beginning, but it is as true as that Tuesday follows Monday and that, barring catastrophe, spring comes around again every year. I ask and I listen when I meet other women who have lost the men they loved, and I know that this is true.

We compromise and we learn to cope, we widows, and in the end we are different women, stronger women, women who come to respect ourselves. It is the gift that comes after the fire.

Sometimes I wonder if Booth would approve of me now, if we should meet again. He liked, in his courtly Texas way, to take care of his women, his wife and daughter. It was the Code of the West. He protected me, even from his own illness, and now I have learned all the realities. No more the child-wife, I have learned how to fight for what I want. I have learned to redefine who I am, give up the role in which I was cast for thirty-one years.

God knows I wish I had him back. I wish he were still sitting across the breakfast table from me, putting Tabasco on his egg, slipping a bit of his toast to Frieda and muttering that the Republicans seem to have botched it again. It would be lovely to lay it all in his lap, know that somebody cares what happens. But failing that, there is me. I am very surprised to see these days that I believe in me.

It takes a lot of doing. Free-lance writers live a notoriously hand-to-mouth existence. The postman may or may not come with a check in time for the taxes; he may deliver a lot of brown envelopes with printed notices saying that the work won't do. When Booth was alive, each one of these rejections was a stab to the ego I nursed in my chest like a physical pain. It was he who taught me to keep at it, refuse to let one failure put me off. Maybe he left me a better inheritance than money.

Before he died we talked about a book I wanted to write about my mother, who died of tuberculosis in an era when the disease was viewed as little better than leprosy. When he died, I lost my editor and literary critic as well as my husband. But there wasn't any answer to that. A year after he died Crowell published *In the Shadow of the White Plague*. Work, as Louis always said, is a great panacea.

"Julia," I said recently to a friend across the coffee cups on the table between us, "what do you hold onto now that Joe is gone?"

With Julia it is her grandchildren. With Dorothy, who nursed a husband with throat cancer for eleven months at home before he died, it is the church. For Sarah, who swallowed a whole bottle of sleeping pills and dove into the lake wearing her coat and her glasses one December night, it was a subsequent autumnal marriage to one of her late husband's old friends, who was likewise widowed.

For me it is simply me. I have come a long way from the moment when I sobbed into the telephone to Ted that I had expected to have to survive without Booth, without money but not without friends, all of whom seemed to be moving away. That was the second valley into which I stumbled in my fight for survival, and now I know that, if I have to, I will make new friends, keep the ties with the old ones stretched but enduring. Friendship means more to me now, and I value it in a special way.

But what I didn't much take notice of at the time were the words Ted used over the telephone wires when the world looked so black and my life so hopeless.

"Mom," he said, horrified to hear me casting aside all semblance of control, pushing him into the role of comforter, shamelessly reversing patterns on which we had both come to count. "Mom," he said, and I could tell

I had violated the boundaries, "you're going to be all right. You're doing a fine job."

And it was then he gave me the Good Housekeeping Seal of Approval, which in my anguish at the time I scarcely noticed.

"I respect what you're doing," he said.

And what was I doing?

Learning to stand alone.